The Guns of Dakar

Books by
JOHN WILLIAMS

History

Heyday for Assassins
Mutiny 1917
The Ides of May
Gallipoli
The Home Fronts, Britain, France, Germany, 1914–1918
The Guns of Dakar

Criminology

Suddenly at The Priory
Hume: Portrait of a Double Murderer

The Guns of Dakar

September 1940

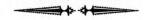

JOHN WILLIAMS

Heinemann : London

William Heinemann Ltd

15 Queen St, Mayfair, London W1X 8BE

LONDON MELBOURNE TORONTO
JOHANNESBURG AUCKLAND

First published 1976
© John Williams 1976
434 86630 x

Printed in Great Britain by
W & J Mackay Limited, Chatham

For
Sonia, once again . . .

CONTENTS

ILLUSTRATIONS

Acknowledgments

Copyright in illustrations 1, 2, 3 and 4, Imperial War Museum.
Illustration 5 copyright Musée de la Guerre, Vincennes/Dorka

FOREWORD

This is the story of Operation Menace, the Anglo-French enterprise of September 1940 primarily designed to win over Dakar, the capital of French West Africa, for the Free French led by General de Gaulle. Dakar, a great seaport and military base situated on the Atlantic coast of Africa, was then, nominally at least, loyal to the French Vichy government, though the strength of this support was doubtful and de Gaulle was firmly convinced he could, by personal persuasion, rally the people of Dakar to the Free French cause. Though initially conceived by de Gaulle, the project was enthusiastically taken up by Winston Churchill, the British Prime Minister, who saw in the gaining of Dakar notable advantages for the British as well as for the Free French. Britain's interest in Dakar stemmed from the fact that if it were to be occupied by the Germans, as well it might while it remained under Vichy control, the vital British sea-route to the Cape and beyond would be gravely threatened.

The United States, too, was concerned about Dakar. A German presence there was seen as a potential danger to American security, more especially as it was the nearest point in Africa to the American continent. So, with the United States as anxious as Britain, and indeed the Free French, to keep the Germans out, there was, in the summer of 1940, considerable vested interest in securing Dakar for the Allies.

Operation Menace was a bold concept, sponsored at a time of great danger and difficulty for Britain. In August 1940, when it was planned and prepared, Hitler's invasion threat was at its height and all the country's scant resources—two months after Dunkirk—were needed for home defence. Nevertheless, even amid the pressing preoccupations of these weeks, Churchill and his War Cabinet colleagues remained determined to go ahead with Menace. They viewed it not only as strategically worth while but as a demonstration—small though it was—that the Allies could strike out from British shores, take an initiative as well as just react after the enemy had struck first.

Unfortunately, Operation Menace turned out to be a fiasco. Instead of the hoped-for quick and unresisted take-over of a friendly Dakar by de Gaulle and his Free French contingent (with British warships and troops, standing by in the background, providing a threat of force in the event of opposition), de Gaulle was humiliatingly rebuffed, the British Navy was drawn in, and the operation dragged into a three-day battle that ended with Dakar untaken and the Anglo-French armada forced to retire in defeat. Over-hasty planning, faulty intelligence, deplorably bad communications and inadequate top-command liaison all contributed to Menace's failure. But it was also dogged by mischance and sheer bad luck. First, there was the unforeseen appearance on the scene of Vichy warships (on a mission unconnected with the defence of Dakar), which disrupted the Menace time-table and jeopardized whatever remaining security it possessed. And second, on Day I of the operation, the Dakar area was blanketed by a totally unexpected fog which fatally hampered visibility.

The net result of all this was a *débâcle* that seriously harmed de Gaulle and his cause—producing a lasting distrust of him in the United States—and had unhappy repercussions for Churchill. The plan that would have been acclaimed as a daring Allied victory if it had succeeded was roundly condemned because it had failed. The advantage of hindsight makes it easy to criticize Operation Menace. Indeed, politically it was a gamble, which might well have caused Vichy France to declare war against Britain, and Germany to occupy North Africa. As a combined operation, undertaken with almost no experience of such actions, it bristled with defects and errors. But, launched as it was in those desperate days when Britain was battling for survival, it was a brave effort to take the war (even if indirectly) into the enemy's camp and pre-empt a possible enemy move in a new theatre that could become important. As such, Operation Menace was not entirely without merit; and at least its very mistakes provided valuable lessons for the conduct of similar operations in the future.

J.W.

ACKNOWLEDGMENTS

I have to thank many people for the help they have given me in writing this book. I am especially grateful to the late General Sir Edward Spears, who allowed me full access to his valuable unpublished Journal of the Dakar Operation. I am also greatly indebted to Major F. Mitchell, M.C., who likewise put at my disposal his personal Diary and much other material and information. Captain P. N. Walter, D.S.O., R.N. (Retd.), gave me much helpful information; as did Mrs Mary Pain, who among other things allowed me access to the Papers of the late Commander M. G. Saunders, R.N. Others who have helped me with recollections, records or other material include: Cmdr W. N. D. Lang, R.N.V.R.; Capt H. Home Cook, R.N. (Retd.); Mr John Stokes, M.P.; Miss J. Eisen; Miss Marjorie Coombs; Mr John St John; Mr T. T. Jenkins; Mr B. G. Gallaway; Mr G. E. Higham; Mr Ingram Watson; Mr Tony Palmer; and Capt. Eric Bush, DSO**, DSC., R.N. (Retd.). I am also indebted to the staffs of the Public Record Office, the Naval Historical Branch of the Ministry of Defence, and the Imperial War Museum Library for help in tracing essential material; and have, as usual, found the resources of the London Library indispensable.

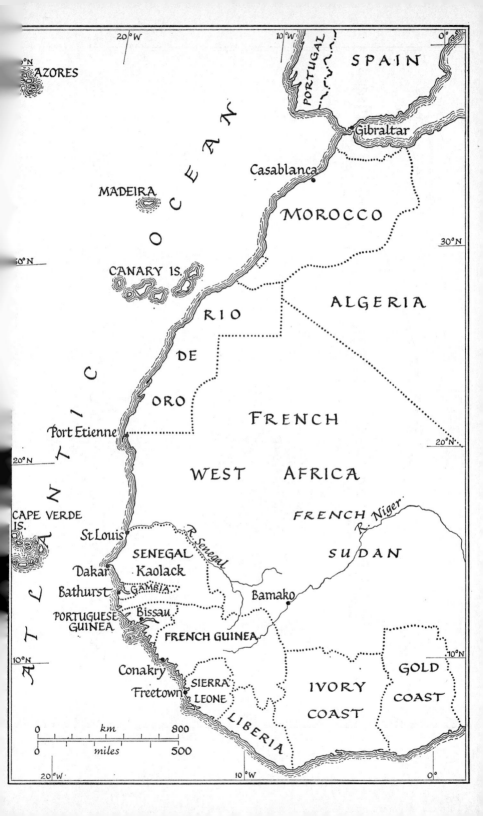

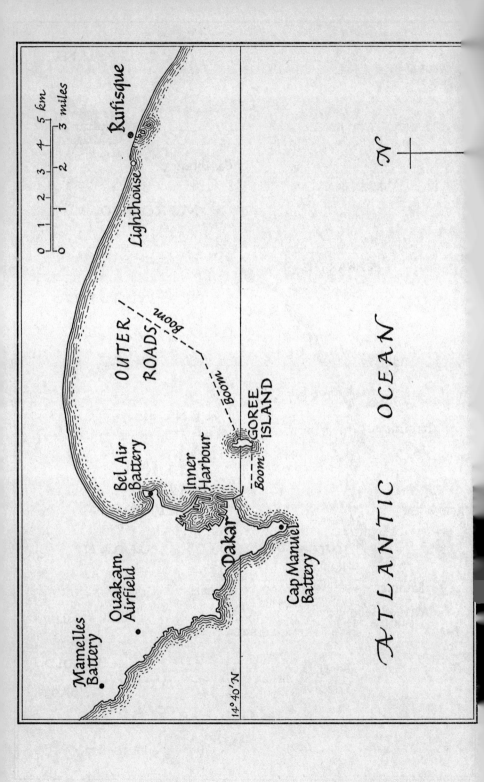

Mamelles Battery

Ouakam Airfield

Bel Air Battery

Inner Harbour

Dakar

Cap Manuel Battery

OUTER ROADS

Boom

Boom

GOREE ISLAND

Boom

Lighthouse

Rufisque

0 1 2 3 4 5 km

0 1 2 3 miles

N

14° 40' N

ATLANTIC OCEAN

CHAPTER I

THE PLAN IS BORN

At the end of August 1940 there sailed from Liverpool, the Clyde and Scapa a motley fleet of warships and transports carrying Free French and British troops, southward bound for French West Africa. Its mission was to win over West Africa's capital, Dakar, for General de Gaulle's newly-created Free French movement. Along with the British admiral commanding and a British general, de Gaulle himself was in the convoy, heading the Free French contingent. The project was code-named Operation Menace, perhaps aptly so in view of de Gaulle's anxiety that this confrontation of Frenchmen by Frenchmen should succeed through threats rather than bloodshed. In those early days of World War Two, when combined operations were a virtually untried tactic, it was a bold and risky enterprise. Britain, having heavily underwritten the project, was keenly anxious for its success, as was benevolently neutral America. For de Gaulle himself the stakes were vital: in gaining Dakar he would take a major step towards establishing his name as Free French leader and confirm the Free French movement as a significant force on the Allied side.

De Gaulle had arrived in England some ten weeks before, in mid-June. Leaving a France stunned and prostrated by defeat, he had presented himself in London as the sole hope of continued French resistance to Germany. He came at a dark and desperate moment for the Free World. In those June days of 1940, in Britain and America as well as France, it did not need a pessimist to believe that Germany had won or was about to win the war. It had taken Hitler's forces just six weeks to shatter the great French Army, overrun half France and reduce much of the country to chaos. Paris was occupied, millions of refugees were on the move, the Government was on the point of collapse and France was about to sign an armistice and place herself under the shaky protection of the aged Marshal Pétain, heading the defeatist Vichy administration. Britain, having by a near miracle saved her army at Dunkirk, was licking her wounds and preparing with woefully inadequate and ill-organized resources to meet the next and most dangerous threat of all: invasion. With France gone, now she stood alone. She might count one blessing denied to France, that she was an island. She had another, that since the end of the 'phoney' war on 10th May she had been under the indomitable leadership of a new Prime Minister, Winston Churchill.

As a little known figure in France, and hardly known at all in Britain, de Gaulle's reception was less than enthusiastic. The British leaders could have wished for a more distinguished personality than this 50-year-old professional soldier, only recently promoted general, who had served briefly in the Government of Paul Reynaud as France slid swiftly towards disaster. General Edward Spears (later Sir Edward), who had escorted de Gaulle to England in one of the last planes out of Bordeaux, seat of Reynaud's disintegrating Government, was reproached by Churchill and others for not bringing over some more influential Frenchman, a politician who could appeal to world opinion and rally potential opposition in France. Spears replied that, so deep had fear and defeatism bitten among the politicians of Bordeaux, there was literally no one else willing to come. Whatever his qualifications or lack of them, de Gaulle was the only one.

In French military circles Charles de Gaulle had been that rather unpopular figure, the junior officer with unconventional ideas. Born in 1890 and in his early days a keen student of history, he had graduated from St Cyr at the age of twenty-two, and fought in the First World War, being wounded three times and captured at Verdun in 1916. To this record as a fighting soldier he was soon adding a reputation—in some quarters, far from favourable—as a military thinker. His captivity had given him time to ponder on what he considered the weaknesses of French strategy; and in the post-war years he had developed strongly-held theories on warfare and the kind of army France needed to ensure her future security. Like Liddell Hart and other pioneers in England, he realized the coming importance in war of tanks and air power. And while the French High Command was placing its faith in static defence as exemplified in the Maginot Line (then building), de Gaulle believed that what was required was a mobile and highly mechanized offensive force, a small professional army as opposed to a large conscript one. His views, propounded in 1934 in his book, *Vers l'Armée de Métier*, provoked strong opposition from many of his superiors and left-wing politicians.

One politician who did support him was Paul Reynaud, then Finance Minister. But Reynaud's attempts to get de Gaulle's ideas implemented by the Chamber were unsuccessful. Increasingly convinced of the correctness of his theories, de Gaulle soldiered on. And the calamitous events of May and June 1940 on the Belgian and French fronts were to prove him only too right. At the start of the war he was a colonel in command of a tank brigade. Then, promoted brigadier-general in May to command the newly-formed 4th Armoured Division, he fought a distinguished action at Abbeville. But within days of this he was to leave the army for a brief participation in politics. On the 5th June Reynaud appointed him Under Secretary of State for War, an office he was to hold for less than a fortnight before leaving his war-torn country to set up his standard of defiance and resistance in England.

In their relations with de Gaulle, Churchill and his colleagues were to find him anything but easy. This toweringly tall, gawky and rather lugubrious Frenchman with the features that were a gift for the cartoonist could be obstinate, prickly, even arrogant, and was liable to stand heavily on his dignity. His austere,

3

aloof manner did not exude or inspire warmth. But he had an almost mystical faith in his destiny as the saviour of France. Once he said quite seriously to a group of friends: 'I really am Joan of Arc.'[1] And his fighting spirit and determination quickly showed themselves in his stirring broadcast appeals to Frenchmen in Britain and overseas to join him in the struggle against Germany. 'The flame of French resistance must not and shall not die,' he proclaimed in his first historic radio appeal on the 18th June.

The immediate results of his call were unimpressive. Initially, a mere few hundred supporters had come forward—just a fraction of the thousands of French servicemen then in England, the great majority of whom were anxious only to get back to France. But soon the numbers grew, rallied by de Gaulle in his visits to the various French transit camps. Among them were officers who would form the nucleus of his Free French movement. However, what disappointed the British Government was his failure to attract any notable French leaders. The French Ambassador in London, M. Corbin, had refused to join him, and General Noguès, Governor-General of French North Africa, had declined de Gaulle's offer to place himself under him if Noguès would keep North Africa in the war. Nor did the Government see de Gaulle accepted as a leader in France, unknown as he was, in the event of any future revolt by the French people. All this caused them to regard the general somewhat uncertainly in these first weeks.

Nevertheless, on 28th June de Gaulle was officially recognized as 'Leader of all Free Frenchmen, wherever they may be, who rally to him in support of the Allied Cause.' A British Mission to the general was appointed, headed by the man who had brought him out of France in the last days of the tottering Reynaud Government, General Edward Spears. Officially named British Military Mission No. 20, this became better known as the Spears Mission. Spears was the best possible choice as the Mission's leader. With an intimate knowledge of France and Frenchmen, he spoke French like a native. He was a forceful character, energetic, outspoken, and exacting in getting things done. He had been at the centre of French affairs in both World Wars. In the first war he had filled various important liaison appointments, ending in 1917 as head of the British Military Mission in Paris. Then, in May 1940, as Winston Churchill's special representative with Reynaud, he had been the vital link between the two Premiers in the disastrous weeks leading to France's defeat. During that time he had first met de Gaulle, newly appointed to Reynaud's Government, and been impressed with him as the only firm and determined man among the Premier's scared and wavering colleagues. He had been able to bring him to England only by a last-minute subterfuge. Pretending to say goodbye to him on the Bordeaux airfield as his plane was about to leave for England, Spears hauled him on to the aircraft just as it was taking off. Even then they were lucky to reach England, for the plane had run out of fuel and had had to land at Jersey to refuel. 'It is interesting to think,' Spears wrote, 'what the course of history might have been had the plane crashed. Nobody at that time would have missed de Gaulle, or me, or the pilot.'*

Despite this official recognition as Free French leader, the Government's backing of de Gaulle did not go very far. He was hampered in his recruiting efforts, and the British even competed with him in enlisting French servicemen in their own forces and attracting French agents for secret missions in France. Spears, struggling with officialdom to obtain help and facilities for de Gaulle, met constant obstruction. 'Day in, day out,' he noted, 'I have fought through the trammels of Departments and fiercely torn down the network of prejudice, hesitation and procrastination . . . I know I have impressed my personality on Whitehall by pushing and shoving.'² A friend told him he had made sixty enemies a day. Among the Service Departments he found he got least co-operation from the Admiralty, where there was a strong bias in favour of the French admirals 'because they were admirals.' The First Sea Lord, Admiral Sir Dudley Pound, would believe no ill of Admiral Darlan, the French Naval Chief,

---

* Among the chief members of Spears' staff were Colonel Williams, his GSO I: Wing-Commander Grinnell-Milne; Commander Younghusband, R. N.; and Captain Mercer-Nairne (later the Marquess of Lansdowne).

despite his joining the Vichy Government.

Not until the 7th August did the Government sign a formal compact with de Gaulle. This, known as the Churchill-de Gaulle agreement, gave the Free French forces national autonomy under British command, guaranteed their expenses pending later repayment by France, promised help to Free Frenchman to obtain British citizenship in case of need and absolved them from the obligation to fight against their fellow-countrymen. It also gave de Gaulle the right to form a 'civil establishment'. So, after nearly two months de Gaulle and his movement were accepted as an Ally. And at last, after making do in various temporary premises, he was installed in a permanent London headquarters at Carlton Gardens, grandly overlooking the Mall.

Perhaps it was just coincidence, but de Gaulle's formal acceptance into the Allied fold closely followed his ultimate condemnation by the Vichy Government. Ever since his departure from France, Pétain and his colleagues had fulminated against de Gaulle as a traitor and deserter, and at the end of June he had been summoned to appear before the Military Tribunal at Toulouse charged with refusal to obey orders 'in the presence of the enemy.' Then in July the Tribunal had proceeded to try him in his absence and condemn him to death, at the same time confiscating his property. The news was made known on 2nd August, five days before the publication of the British agreement. De Gaulle was unperturbed, seeing the sentence as an inevitable move by Vichy to distract attention from its own 'evil actions'. And to confirm his new allegiance, at the end of August his Free French army was ceremonially inspected by King George VI.

The Free French forces de Gaulle now commanded comprised units from Norway, a brigade of Chasseurs Alpins, two Foreign Legion battalions and some hundreds of sailors—in all about 7,000 men, less than half of whom were fighting personnel. He could also count on a few ships and aircraft. He had now gathered round him at Carlton Gardens a body of close associates. His *chef de cabinet* was Geoffroy de Courcel; and his service staff and colleagues included Admiral Emile Muselier, his deputy; Colonel de Larminat; Commandant Thierry d'Argenlieu; Major Brosset; Captain Philippe de Hautecloque (the future General Leclerc); Lieutenant Hettier de Bois-lambert; and Captain Dewavrin (also known as 'Passy'). Among his civilian colleagues were René Pleven; Professor Cassin; Georges Boris; Pierre-Olivier Lapie; Jean Oberlé; Jean Marin; and Maurice Schumann. Some of these names would figure prominently in de Gaulle's forthcoming moves to take the Free French standard overseas.

De Gaulle had insisted from the first that 'France had lost only a campaign, and not a war.' He refused to consider France as a beaten nation while her fleet and her Empire, ranging over parts of India and the Pacific and vast tracts of Africa, remained intact. But in the immediate aftermath of France's defeat the French Fleet was a dubious asset. Though the armistice terms provided that it would not be used by the Germans, the British Government could not afford to trust the enemy pledge. It was seen that the powerful French battleships, if taken over by the Germans, would give the enemy a dangerous naval superiority. The War Cabinet therefore decided—and for Churchill it was one of the hardest decisions of the war—that the French Fleet must be eliminated. The French ships in British ports and at Alexandria were neutralised without much difficulty, but at Mers-el-Kebir, near Oran, where the main force was based, the French naval commander, General Gensoul, refused to accept the British ultimatum. On 3rd July a British force from Gibraltar under Admiral Sir James Somerville bombarded the French Fleet, destroying two battleships and a battlecruiser and killing some 1,300 French officers and sailors. The Vichy Government reacted bitterly and broke off diplomatic relations. De Gaulle, to do him credit, accepted the blow as 'an urgent and terrible necessity', even though it gravely harmed his cause among Frenchmen and shocked many of them, potential re-cruits, into changing their minds about joining him.

But with or without the fleet, there was still the Empire. And as a first token of imperial resistance, on 20th July the distant

New Hebrides, in the Pacific, declared for the Free French leader. But de Gaulle had his eyes on Africa. Surveying the map of Africa, he determined that it was from here that France must continue the fight. France's African possessions would provide a base for recruiting an army, maintaining French sovereignty and—one day—getting back into Europe. Between them these possessions covered a huge area: French North Africa, French Equatorial Africa, French West Africa. Among all these far-flung dominions, the problem was where to start.

There was little hope of planting the Free French flag in the North African bloc of Morocco, Algeria and Tunisia. Just across the Mediterranean, it was too exposed to the risk of German occupation. The authority of the Vichy Government was strong there, the people had little stomach for resistance and the Mers-el-Kebir episode still rankled bitterly. French Equatorial Africa and the Cameroons, remote from the war and its effects, offered better prospects. Soon after France's defeat de Gaulle had received encouraging messages from various centres where pro-Free French demonstrations had occurred. It was thus at the Equatorial bloc that he directed his first efforts. Early in August he sent out four trusted agents to Lagos, in Nigeria, charged to move through the territories and rally supporters: Hettier de Boislambert, 'a small man,' in the description of Spears, 'with a heart so big you wondered it could be contained in his short frame, extremely brave, perfectly loyal and very intelligent';[3] Commandant de Hautecloque, a regular cavalry officer who was to become well known as General Leclerc; Major Parant; and René Pleven. They were well received and after various hazardous adventures were to succeed in rallying the French Cameroons, along with which, in quick succession; the Chad territory, the Congo and Ubangi were to declare themselves for de Gaulle. Only the Gabon stood out: a brief rising in his favour here was quickly suppressed by Vichy interests.

French West Africa, comprising the colonies of Senegal, Sudan, Guinea, the Ivory Coast and Dahomey, was a tougher proposition than the Equatorial bloc. Here the pro-Vichy authority was more firmly established, and closely linked with

that of North Africa. It also possessed considerable military resources. But, with North Africa ruled out, West Africa had all
along been de Gaulle's primary target for a Free French *coup*.
In particular he was interested in its capital, Dakar. Standing on
the Cape Verde peninsula in Senegal, strongly fortified, posses-
sing the best harbour on the west coast of Africa between
Casablanca and Cape Town, and with its international airfield,
Dakar was the starting-point of the shortest trans-Atlantic route
to South America. It was a powerful naval base equipped with
marine arsenal, large drydock and destroyer basin, a great commercial port and the seat of the Governor-General of French
West Africa. In short, it was for de Gaulle a glittering prize both
strategically and from the prestige angle. And he believed he
would find a strong body of support there from anti-Vichy elements.

Winston Churchill had heard about the Dakar idea, apparently from de Gaulle himself, by the beginning of July. He
had mentioned it at a War Cabinet meeting on the 5th, when he
said that General Spears was interviewing de Gaulle to find out
'whether he was prepared to put ashore somewhere behind
Dakar with a view to rallying French forces.'[4] Soon after, at a
meeting at Carlton Gardens, de Gaulle announced his plan to
his staff. He declared that if they wanted to bring France back
into the war and worthily represent her interests, it was vitally
important that the seat of the (Free) French Government that
continued the struggle should be based on French soil. It was
imperative too for the Government to choose a centre that by its
size and reputation symbolized the essential France. 'That is
why I've decided,' he said, 'and the information I possess shows
me it is possible—to establish the capital of the Empire in arms
at Dakar.'[5]

Not all his staff were convinced. Dewavrin pointed out that
it would be impossible to hold West Africa unless they controlled North Africa at the same time. De Gaulle replied that
there was no question of action against North Africa, as General
Noguès refused to co-operate unless ten divisions were sent him
from England. But there were the desert and the mountains be-

tween Dakar and North Africa, and it was vital for them to instal themselves on French soil as soon as possible. 'So, gentlemen, we are going to leave for Dakar with all the French troops we can arm and equip here. I have spoken with Mr Churchill. Get to work so that we may be ready to leave within four to six weeks.'[6]

De Gaulle's first scheme for gaining Dakar involved a landing well to the south of it, at Konakri, in French Guinea. From Konakri he would work his way up country to Dakar, rallying adherents and native troops as he went. The capital, approached from the rear, would then fall to him like a ripe plum. At Carlton Gardens he outlined his plan to his staff with the aid of a large-scale map of West Africa. 'I do not know Africa at all,' he said, 'but we have men who do. And from what they tell me it would seem that Konakri will be the best place to land.'[7] In theory, Konakri had certain advantages. Only some 100 miles from the British base of Freetown, in Sierra Leone, it had a small port, an airfield and a serviceable railway. Troops, light tanks and transport could be landed there, along with aircraft. And Intelligence suggested that Guinea would welcome the Free French. The whole operation would be bloodless—something on which de Gaulle always insisted—and accomplished by peaceful persuasion.

But however inviting the Konakri plan looked on paper, it was in fact highly impractical. It badly underestimated the difficulties de Gaulle's force would meet in its trek through rough and unfamiliar African territory. And it ignored the strength of Vichy opposition likely to be found at Dakar itself, especially after the traumatic Mers-el-Kebir episode of early July. About this, however, de Gaulle had second thoughts. Accepting the possibility of a sea-borne intervention from Dakar, he realized he would need naval help, and would have to rely on the protective cover of the British Navy.

Late in July de Gaulle put his scheme to the Prime Minister. Churchill listened non-committally. But by now, amid all his other preoccupations he was vitally interested in Dakar. A problem for the Cabinet had all along been how best to employ de

Gaulle and his 7,000-strong Free French contingent that was kicking its heels in English camps at Aldershot and Liverpool, waiting for action. Ministers had welcomed his plans to rally the African colonies, and especially those of West Africa, bordering the Atlantic. Churchill had first considered a Free French move against Casablanca, in Morocco, but when this was seen to be too strongly entrenched in the North African bloc, he had turned to Dakar. The possession of Dakar would be a powerful gain for the British as well as the Free French. Not only was it the nearest point in Africa to South America, but its use by the Germans as a naval and air base would gravely imperil Britain's trans-Atlantic shipping routes and communications with her West African colonies and the Far East.

The Chiefs of Staff had already stressed this danger in an appreciation that they had produced on 16th July, on the implications of French hostility. In this they had even proposed that plans should be made for the destruction of Dakar's naval base by naval action. But a fortnight later they agreed that naval bombardment was ruled out as being counter to Government policy not to damage Anglo-French relations. They also submitted that a landing against French opposition would be an operation of some magnitude for which British forces were not then available. At the same time the Colonial Office was pointing to alternatives to military action. In a memorandum dated 3rd August it reported its attempts, after the defeat of France, to persuade the French colonies to continue fighting as Britain's allies. However, though Free French elements were found that were ready to rally to the allied side, they were being silenced and rendered inoperative by strong Vichy pressure. The Colonial Office therefore proposed that, as the use of military force was rejected, Britain's policy should be to strengthen and encourage these anti-Vichy elements wherever possible.[8]

If effective, this policy would greatly aid de Gaulle's plans for a bloodless occupation of Dakar. But how far Vichy control could be neutralized by the rallying of pro-Free French forces, at Dakar or anywhere else, remained to be seen. And there were not only the Vichy authorities to be considered. Theoretically, the Germans had access to Dakar through the agency of the German Armistice Commission. And their presence there would effectively rule out any pro-Gaullist activities.

The start of August saw swift moves in the development of the Dakar project. From then until the end of the month it was to be planned, re-planned, altered, enlarged and pressed forward with an almost hectic urgency. Rarely during the war can an operation have emerged from the drawing-board into its final form with such speed—or it may be, with such haste. Throughout those August weeks—weeks in which Britain was facing the imminent threat of invasion and mustering all her resources to meet the threat—hardly a day passed without a conference, consultation or meeting that produced some decision about it. It was constantly on the agenda of every executive or planning body from the War Cabinet downwards: the Chiefs of Staff Committee, the Vice-Chiefs of Staff, the Inter-Service Planning Staff, the Service Departments, the Directorate of Operations, the operation's Joint Commanders, de Gaulle, General Spears and the Free French staff. And behind the whole project, as it went from stage to stage, was the driving force of Winston Churchill.

De Gaulle's scheme for a landing at Konakri with British naval help had been quickly abandoned as unworkable. Meanwhile an outline plan for Free French action in West Africa, including the occupation of Dakar, had been produced by de Gaulle, General Spears and Major Desmond Morton, Churchill's Personal Assistant, working together at Churchill's request. On 3rd August Churchill gave this plan his general approval. The Chiefs of Staff Committee was now brought in. On the 4th it drafted a report on the plan for the War Cabinet, based on three assumptions: the operating force must be equipped to land in any French West African port; it should comprise only Free French troops, with British co-operation confined to ships and naval escort; to facilitate an unopposed landing, the operation should be 'as between Frenchmen'. Further, the Free French contingent should number about 2,500 men, composed of two battalions, a company of tanks, artillery and engineer units and a bomber and fighter flight, of which the British would provide the Hurricanes. It was first estimated this force could be ready at Aldershot by 10th August and could sail from Liverpool between the 13th and 23rd, arriving at Dakar on 28th August (or other ports a few days later).[9]

On the 5th August the War Cabinet considered the COS report and a memorandum on the project by Churchill.[10] Churchill urged that Free French action overseas should be given 'every encouragement'. Various operations had been considered, and it was de Gaulle's opinion that the most advantageous would be a landing in one of the West African colonies. The Prime Minister then submitted the provisional plan, by which de Gaulle would be ready to sail for West Africa on 15th August, 'with a view to hoisting the Free French flag in the French territories in West Africa, the occupation of Dakar and the consolidation under the Free French flag of the French colonies in West and Equatorial Africa.' Reactions to this grandiose-sounding proposal were mixed. Some Ministers doubted de Gaulle's ability to make an unopposed landing—especially at Dakar, with its strong defences. Mr A. V. Alexander, First Lord of the Admiralty, emphasized that as the British would be providing the naval escort, any attempt by the Vichy French to stop the expedition would provoke an Anglo-French naval action. But doubts and objections were overridden and the operation—to be known as 'Scipio'—agreed in principle, with stress laid on the vital need for secrecy.

Later that day, however, misgivings were voiced at a Chiefs of Staff meeting. The Chiefs had initially had doubts about the operation because of its possible effect on Anglo-Vichy relations. Now, on realizing that de Gaulle had made no allowance for naval intervention by Vichy, their worries were increased. This would, as they told Churchill, involve a heavier and more extended British commitment than had been foreseen—a serious matter at this time when British resources were so severely strained.

But the more the Prime Minister had been considering the

project, the more his enthusiasm for it had grown. He had always relished the kind of military operation that needed daring and surprise, involved some risk, and gave hopes of opening a new and unexpected 'front'. And just as in World War I he had eagerly sponsored the Dardanelles expedition, so now this Dakar enterprise fired his aggressive imagination. By the 6th August, when he saw de Gaulle again, he had conjured up a vivid picture of how the operation would proceed. The general has told how he was shown into the Cabinet Room at No. 10 on whose big table maps were spread out.[11] Pacing up and down, Churchill addressed him animatedly. 'We must,' he began, 'together gain control of Dakar.' He explained that this was vital for both France and Britain. After discussions with the Admiralty and Chiefs of Staff, he could tell de Gaulle that Britain was prepared to assist in the expedition. A substantial naval force was being allocated to it, but could not stay long off the African coast as other tasks awaited it. The action therefore must be quick. De Gaulle's plan for Konakri had on examination proved impracticable, but, said the Prime Minister, he had an alternative proposal. Then, in true Churchillian style, he launched into a graphic description.

'Dakar wakes up one morning,' he told de Gaulle, 'sad and uncertain. But behold, by the light of the rising sun, its inhabitants perceive the sea, to a great distance, covered with ships. An immense fleet! A hundred war or transport vessels! These approach slowly, addressing by radio messages of friendship to the town, to the Navy, to the Garrison. Some of them are flying the tricolour. The others are sailing under the British, Dutch, Polish or Belgian colours. From this Allied force there breaks away an inoffensive small ship bearing the white flag of parley. It enters the port and disembarks the envoys of General de Gaulle. These are brought to the Governor. Their job is to convince him that, if he lets you land, the Allied fleet retires, and that nothing remains but to settle, between him and you, the terms of his co-operation. On the contrary, if he wants a fight, he has every chance of being crushed.'

Swept on by his own eloquence, Churchill continued: 'During this conversation between the Governor and your representatives, Free French and British aircraft are flying peacefully over the town, dropping friendly leaflets. The military and the civilians, among whom your agents are at work, are discussing passionately among themselves the advantages offered by an arrangement with you and the drawbacks presented, on the contrary, by a large-scale battle fought against those who, after all, are the Allies of France. The Governor feels that, if he resists, the ground will give way under his feet. You will see that he will go on with the talks till they reach a satisfactory conclusion. Perhaps meanwhile he will wish, "for honour's sake", to fire a few shots. But he will not go farther. And that evening he will dine with you and drink to the final victory.'

It was a heady and seductive picture, presented with all the force of Churchill's rolling phrases and dramatic gestures. De Gaulle, discounting the colourful trimmings, realised the sound thinking behind it. Though Churchill now proposed a strongly *Anglo*-French, as opposed to an entirely or largely French operation—with the possible use of force—the general saw no real alternative to it. The Free French could not win Dakar by themselves. And if they declined British help and abandoned the plan, sooner or later the British would need for strategic reasons to seize the port on their own. The resulting violence and destruction would only increase Vichy enmity to Britain and gravely harm the Free French cause. So, after brief consideration, de Gaulle returned to Downing Street to tell Churchill he accepted the plan.

But the Chiefs of Staff were still not happy. At a meeting held late on 7th August under Churchill's chairmanship, it was agreed that Dakar was the best landing-place for de Gaulle's forces. But after Churchill had asked for an amended plan to provide for increased participation of British troops, the Chiefs pointed out certain risks: that British attempts to rally the French colonies might halt any improvement of Anglo-Vichy relations; and that de Gaulle's Free French movement might provoke war with Vichy France and the French colonies. They did, however, agree that the operation should go ahead, provided agents' reports from Dakar showed substantial support for de Gaulle.[12]

But Churchill was now determined that Dakar must be taken —with or without resistance. Early on the 8th he issued a memorandum to General Ismay, in which he stressed the importance to Britain of de Gaulle's gaining Dakar at the earliest moment. If his emissaries reported that it could not be taken unopposed, a suitable British and Polish force should be provided, with full naval protection. The operation once begun, must be pushed through. The Chiefs of Staff were to be instructed to draft a plan to take the port. For this they should have available de Gaulle's forces and any obtainable French warships, a British naval force adequate to handle Vichy warships and cover the landing, a Polish brigade, a Royal Marines brigade or alternatively a commando contingent, and suitable air support. The plan was to be prepared forthwith. 'Time is vital,' wrote Churchill.

De Gaulle's original scheme for Dakar as a purely Free French operation had now rapidly ballooned into a joint action with heavy British naval and military commitment—and under British command. For to lead the expedition Churchill now approved the appointment of Vice-Admiral John Cunningham, C.B., M.V.O., commanding the 1st Cruiser Squadron,* and Major-General Noel Irwin, C.B., D.S.O., M.C., commanding the 2nd Division, Home Forces. Cunningham—'the quickest brain at sea with the possible exception of Vian,' as his future Chief Staff Officer, Captain Walter, described him, 'and a man who didn't suffer fools gladly'—left the cruiser *Devonshire*, at Greenock, on the morning of the 12th August for the Admiralty, to be told he was to command the naval forces for an operation to occupy Dakar. Its object, he was informed, was 'to install de Gaulle and the Free French forces in Dakar in order to hoist the Free French flag in French West Africa and rally the French colonies there to his standard.'[13] General Irwin had been similarly briefed, and that night the two commanders-designate met for the first time.

Thus suddenly plunged into command of the Dakar opera-

* Later Admiral of the Fleet Sir John Cunningham, G.C.B., M.V.O.

tion, next morning Cunningham and Irwin attended a meeting of the Chiefs of Staff Committee. All they had to go on at that stage was a plan for Dakar's capture prepared by the Inter-Services Planning Staff on the 9th. This specified the landing of British troops at six beaches on Cape Verde peninsula, after which—if it was successful—de Gaulle's forces would land. A significant paragraph in the plan ran as follows: 'If Dakar were defended by a resolute commander with alert and determined troops, we consider that the chance of success would be small. In view, however, of the reports of morale at Dakar we consider that this operation might be carried out by highly trained British forces . . . provided total surprise could be achieved.'[14] Nevertheless the ISPS was chary of elaborating the plan before more information was obtained of the actual situation at Dakar. This, it was hoped, would be provided by two British officers, Commander Rushbrooke, R.N., who until recently had been naval liaison officer at Dakar, and Captain Poulter, military liaison officer at Dakar up to July. These officers had been ordered to return to London forthwith and report.

At noon on the 13th Churchill put a revised Dakar plan to the War Cabinet.[15] Now to be code-named Operation Menace, it was designed to install de Gaulle at Dakar backed by British support. Troops stationed there were thought to total some 2,500 Senegalese, with about 200 French officers. If they resisted, Churchill estimated that the Allied force would be sufficient to overpower them. The whole action was to be executed between dawn and dusk. As to the Vichy Government declaring war as a result of it, this was unlikely, said Churchill. Nor would it matter greatly if they did. Only one Cabinet member had reservations. Lord Halifax, Foreign Secretary, was concerned about how Vichy would react, and asked for 24 hours to study the matter. Subject to this the War Cabinet approved the Prime Minister's plan.

On the 14th Cunningham and Irwin—now officially the Joint Commanders—met de Gaulle and Spears at the Admiralty for a preliminary discussion. And that evening they were entertained to dinner by Churchill. The Prime Minister, in

Cunningham's words, 'explained the great results on the general prosecution of the war that might be expected to result from a successful outcome of the enterprise.'[16] He was at pains to impress the commanders that they were concerned only with the military aspects of Menace, and assured them of his full backing whatever the political results. This assurance he was to repeat twice before the expedition sailed.

CHAPTER II

'THIS DOUBTFUL AND COMPLEX AFFAIR'

As Churchill wrote about Menace: 'I had now become set upon this venture.' He clearly saw its risks, the gravest of which, win or lose, was prolonged fighting. But Britain at that moment was living amid far greater dangers. Across the Straits Hitler was preparing imminent invasion. Over England's skies the Battle of Britain was raging as the Luftwaffe strove to destroy the RAF. Channel convoys were being attacked, and docks and airfields being heavily bombed. These and a host of other urgent matters were the daily pre-occupation of the War Cabinet as they studied the Dakar plan. High among the current problems was the threat to Egypt by Mussolini's armies, calling for the hard decision to send General Wavell, the British commander, half Britain's scanty stock of tanks. Compared with this the Dakar operation was, as Churchill admitted, 'a pup'. But whatever its scale he was convinced of its tremendous possibilities. It could secure not only Dakar but the French colonial Empire. And it gave a chance to strike, to show the twin flags of Britain and Free France, to win back a little sorely needed British prestige, when there was precious little opportunity elsewhere.

The broad lines of the operation were now being worked out between de Gaulle, Spears, Admiral Cunningham and General Irwin, meeting in deepest secrecy at the Admiralty. Great efforts were made to conceal de Gaulle's presence there, for fear of leakages. Spears, as head of the British Mission to de Gaulle, was in close and constant touch with him in these weeks. He was impressed with his 'enormous capacity for working miracles' and 'willingness to gamble for enormous stakes.' And in contrast to his reputation for stubbornness, Spears found him refreshingly willing to listen to him and take his advice. But despite the top priority accorded to Operation Menace, the fullest Anglo-French co-operation was lacking. As the scheme developed and planning passed into the hands of the multifarious other bodies, de Gaulle and Spears were kept largely in the dark as to what was happening. They were being left in no doubt that Menace was now predominantly a British 'show'.

But lack of liaison was apparent at Free French headquarters too, along with a growing friction between de Gaulle and his deputy, Admiral Muselier. According to Muselier, de Gaulle had agreed to the stepping-up of Menace into a full dress Anglo-French expedition without consulting his own colleagues:[1] Muselier—a rakish, piratical-looking and highly controversial figure, more noted for his hatred of Vichy's Admiral Darlan than for his love of the Free French movement—had meanwhile produced his own plan for Menace. This involved a Dakar-bound force of three sloops under his command (Force M) leaving a detachment of French troops at Port Etienne (450 miles north of Dakar) to cut Dakar's communications with North Africa, before joining the main convoy at Dakar. Then, in the event of Menace being abandoned en route because of unfavourable reports from Dakar, he would sail on south to Pointe Noire, in Equatorial Africa. After asking—to Muselier's surprise—where Pointe Noire was, de Gaulle accepted the plan and ordered Muselier to hurry on preparations for it.

Muselier understood that, as de Gaulle's deputy, he was to accompany the expedition and command Force M. His staff was immersed in the arrangements when suddenly de Gaulle told him he was not to take part. He wished Muselier to remain in charge of affairs in London while he, de Gaulle, was away. Highly indignant at thus being shunted out, Muselier, in company with the captains of the sloops *Commandant Duboc* and *Commandant Dominé*, bearded de Gaulle and offered to return his admiral's stars and carry on as a frigate commander instead. De Gaulle firmly refused, and from that point he took over from Muselier the supervision of all preparations for Operation Menace, replacing him, as the expedition's second in command, with Commander Thierry d'Argenlieu.

For a professional sailor d'Argenlieu had had an unusual career. He had left the Navy soon after the First World War to become a monk, rejoined it in 1939 and escaped to England the following June after the capture of Cherbourg. Securing demobilisation in July from the French Naval Mission in London, he had entered the Carmelite Order at Kensington, and left it soon after to join the Free French, serving first as a chaplain. As one of de Gaulle's most trusted colleagues, he was appointed to the *Conseil Supérieur* of the Free French Navy; and in the forthcoming operation he was to be chosen to lead the Free French delegation to the authorities at Dakar.

An immediate problem for the Joint Commanders was the assembling of a headquarters staff. So hastily had they been appointed that they had to start work without a staff establishment. Cunningham's Chief Staff Officer was appointed on the 18th, in the person of Captain P. N. Walter, D.S.O. (Cunningham's normal CSO was also captain of the flagship and would thus not be able to supervise the planning of a combined operation.) Irwin found himself so busy that he had to leave the task of staff selection to the War Office. His staff, headed by Lt-Colonel Smith-Hill, began to arrive in driblets around mid-August. This piecemeal recruitment had its drawbacks, as none of the officers had worked together before. The combined staff was allotted Rooms 97 and 98 in the Admiralty. Working conditions were crude. Space was cramped, there were not enough desks, and the staff, as Smith-Hill noted, was always 'in a hurry' coping with the frequent changes of plan and the constant flow of reports and directives. Working to the brief of the rough scheme produced by the ISPS, the officers knew little or nothing of the political background to Menace, and were handicapped by lack of proper tactical intelligence (as to presence of surf, availability of landing places and weather conditions). Cunningham and Irwin occupied Room 99, overlooking the Admiralty quadrangle. Here they spent long hours in conference with de Gaulle and Spears, with Captain Walter and Lt-Colonel Smith-Hill in attendance.

De Gaulle himself was still weighing up the options open to him. On the 19th August he set out his thoughts in a Note.[2] Information from Dakar, he wrote, suggested that service elements there were 'considerably disorganized,' opinion in the town was confused though it was certain that many people disapproved of the armistice, and there was strong anxiety about the food situation. He stressed the vital necessity of avoiding violence. The operation should be regarded as feasible only after Free French servicemen had occupied the chief points of the town and warships in the harbour, and the purely French nature of the enterprise had been clearly announced by leaflets and other means. The take-over must then be executed with the utmost speed. If conditions made this impossible, de Gaulle mooted an alternative plan for a French landing at St Louis, 100 miles north of Dakar, covered by British troops. The French would then march on Dakar, 'negotiating with the authorities and influencing the population.'

But despite the intensive consultations and conferences of these mid-August weeks, the finalized planning of Operation Menace was making little progress. Then, on the 20th, after various revised and modified schemes had been considered, came a decision that threw everything into the melting-pot. The Vice-Chiefs of Staff agreed that the plan approved by the War Cabinet on 13th August for full British participation was impracticable. There were too many difficulties, tactical, logistical and topographical.[3] On Churchill's recommendation, the British commanders and de Gaulle were referred back to de Gaulle's original plan—for a Free French operation with minor British participation. Yet that same day Churchill was still relying on the ultimate sanction of British guns. He made this clear when, presiding over a COS meeting, also attended by de Gaulle, he summed up his own ideas for Menace as a powerful Anglo-French enterprise. '. . . If determined opposition was met with,' he concluded, 'the British forces would use all means to break down resistance.'[4]

Next day, at a top-level meeting, the whole plan was re-examined and virtually finalized. It was none too soon, for under movement orders previously issued, warships and transports for the expedition were already en route towards the chosen embarkation points. As to the vexed question of command, it was now agreed that while Admiral Cunningham and General Irwin should jointly command the expedition, they would not give orders to the Free French without de Gaulle's consent and, save in exceptional circumstances, de Gaulle would exercise no authority over the British forces. Orders from Cunningham to the Free French ships were to be counter-signed by de Gaulle.

De Gaulle was now busy organizing the French resources for Menace. He was able to muster three sloops: the *Savorgnan de Brazza* (1,900 tons), the *Commandant Duboc* and the *Commandant Domine* (both 600 tons), together with two armed trawlers, the *Vaillant* and the *Viking*. There were also two liners borrowed from the Dutch, the *Pennland* and the *Westernland* (both 16,000 tons) and four cargo boats, the *Anadyr*, *Casamance*, *Fort-Lamy* and *Nevada*, to carry the tanks, guns, aircraft in crates, vehicles and provisions. The Free French troops for Menace, to be carried in the *Pennland* and *Westernland*, amounted to a battalion of the Foreign Legion, a company of recruits, a Marine company, a tank company, an artillery battery and ancillary services; in all some 2,500 men, along with the crews of two air squadrons.

The French had no suitable aircraft of their own. But de Gaulle was able to obtain from the Air Ministry six Blenheims and twelve Lysanders. A fortnight's intensive training in flying these, and in dismantling and reassembling them, was provided for the French by RAF instructors. There was, however, another aircraft problem: planes were needed for the proposed landing, early in the operation, of Free French representatives at Dakar's airfield. These, it was decided must be French and have French markings. But no such aircraft could be found. Then, after a belated search, two suitable planes—small biplane two-seater

Lucioles—were discovered in crates at a maintenance depot in Wales. These were hastily assembled, and arrangements made to fly them to Scotland and put them aboard the cruiser *Fiji*, one of the vessels detailed to escort the Dakar-bound Menace convoy.[5]

Admiral Muselier, though excluded by de Gaulle from taking any part in Operation Menace—'My advice was never asked,' he complained—was watching the build-up with a critical eye. And he was quick to give his chief his views about it. He it was who urged de Gaulle to engage Dutch liners as troop transports, in place of the dangerously slower ships the general had initially allotted. And—with some sense—he questioned the inclusion of tanks in what was intended to be a bloodless and peaceful operation. He also protested when de Gaulle allegedly declared to him that if there were resistance he would withdraw and hand over the operation to the British. On no account should the British be allowed to occupy French territory, objected the admiral. And, according to Muselier, it was on his insistence that de Gaulle agreed to send envoys with truce flags into Dakar before any troops landed from the waiting convoy.

De Gaulle regretted that his forces available for Menace were 'so meagre'. He was also disappointed at the size of the British naval contribution, suspecting the Chiefs of Staff of scaling down the original allotment (probably because they were less enthusiastic about Menace than Churchill). Even so, considering the many other urgent calls then being made upon the Navy, the British provision was not unimpressive. It comprised at this stage two battleships, the *Barham* and the *Resolution*, each with 8 15-inch and 12 6-inch guns, four cruisers, the carrier *Ark Royal* with its 32 aircraft, ten destroyers and a tanker. In addition, four transports were to carry the British contingent of four Marine battalions, together with stores and equipment. (The plan to include Polish troops was now cancelled.)

Churchill had constantly stressed the dangers of delay. But with planning and preparation for Menace proving much more complex than anticipated, precious time was slipping by, making nonsense of the original time-table. The first proposed

sailing date, 15th August—envisaging the actual striking date
of the operation as 8th September—had passed with no sign of
readiness. By 20th August the striking date had been postponed
to 18th September. Allowing some three weeks for the voyage
to Dakar, the sailing date could not now be before the end of
August. This left only some ten days for the completion of all
planning and arrangements. One difficulty had arisen in relation to the cargo boats. They were already being loaded when
it was realized that, at $7\frac{1}{2}$ knots, they would be too slow to reach
the appointed rendezvous at the time arranged. But as re-
loading on to faster ships would only have caused further delay,
the slow boats were retained. By Cunningham's orders dated
23rd August the vessels concerned—the *Anadyr*, *Fort-Lamy*,
Nevada, *Casamance* and an English petrol tanker—were to leave
Liverpool on the 26th, five days before the main convoy. They
were to be accompanied by the French vessels *Savorgnan de
Brazza* and *Président Houduce*.

But other troubles had contributed to the delays. In protest
against not being paid for three months, the French crews had
mutinied and armed guards had to be placed on the ships.
After this things had taken an almost comic-opera turn. The
crews refused to sail unless their rations included champagne
and *pâté de foie gras*. ('Some adjustment was made to their
rations,' cryptically states a report.) Then, to add a final touch
of farce, one of the captains had lost his mistress and declined
to leave without her. And when the convoy finally sailed, two
ships collided in the Mersey and both had to return to Liverpool for repairs.[6]

One threat always liable to endanger Menace was leakage
of information. Now, it seemed, this threat had materialized.
Security among the British had been strict: few outside the
senior commanders and planning staffs knew more than that
some operation, possibly in the tropics or Near East, was brew-
ing. If troops had been seen wearing tropical kit, this was good
cover for an expedition to almost any hot country. But among
the Free French forces there had been careless talk. In London
and Liverpool bars the word Dakar was frequently heard as

Frenchmen speculated loudly where this operation for which they were detailed was likely to be. At dinner in a smart London restaurant a party of French officers enthusiastically drank a champagne toast to 'Dakar!' Worse still, de Gaulle himself, when buying a tropical outfit at a well-known store in Piccadilly, was heard to remark that his destination was West Africa. And in August the lorry-loads of assault landing-craft travelling north to Liverpool advertised to everyone that some overseas operation was imminent. Moreover the Dakar 'secret' was said to be well known to officers of the Vichy French Mission still in England who, according to Churchill, passed on the information to members of the Vichy consulates in London and Liverpool. 'We were all in our wartime infancy,' wrote Churchill. 'The sealing of the Island was not to be compared with what we achieved later in the supreme operations of Torch and Overlord.'

The matter of leakages and bad security before Dakar was to become a wartime legend. In the aftermath of Menace it was to be claimed that they were largely responsible for its failure. 'It was clear that leakage of information had undoubtedly taken place through French sources,' stated an official report in late September.[8] No doubt news about the coming operation seeped out fairly widely, but there is no evidence that it reached Vichy. If it did, it was not acted upon. Vichy took no steps to prevent the Menace convoy reaching Dakar, and appeared completely surprised when the operation was launched. It remains a mystery how the 'secret' never got to France. But at the time its exposure was a risk that the British authorities had to take very seriously.

Consequently when reports about leakages reached Lord Halifax, the Foreign Secretary, he passed them on to the Chiefs of Staff. Considering them at a meeting on the 22nd August, the Chiefs decided that, despite the risks involved, the planning for Menace should go ahead.[9] But one of the Joint Commanders was gravely worried on other grounds. General Irwin had strong misgivings about the military aspects of Menace. He recorded his views in a memorandum which the VCIGS,

General Haining, circulated on the 26th.[10] In this Irwin pointed out that the military plan and the allocation of British forces for it were based on only local opposition, and that a miscalculation could have serious results. He was extremely apprehensive about the effect on the population and garrison of a heavy attack by British forces, and thought it highly doubtful that de Gaulle would receive a friendly welcome if he landed behind British guns and bayonets. The British air forces, he thought, would be inadequate in the face of full-scale opposition; and he stressed the insufficiency of assault landing-craft and the troops' inexperience in their use.* Finally, said Irwin, as the object was to make the British force as mobile as possible to meet any situation that might arise, no plans had been made for specific operations. This was largely due to the 'urgency' with which the expedition was organized.

In Irwin's view (as he was later to comment) the project was suffering particularly from over-hasty preparation and lack of information about Dakar itself.[11] But he was equally worried over the training arrangements. The four battalions of Royal Marines detailed for Menace had been switched at short notice from another projected operation against the Cape Verde Islands. And as late as the 24th August three of them were sent to Scapa for a four-day crash course in making opposed beach landings. But training was severely hampered by lack of assault landing-craft. As Lt. A. C. Palmer, of the 1st Battalion, Royal Marines, recalls, his men had to make do with hand-propelled lifeboats. Irwin himself was able to pay them a flying visit only on the 26th—meeting for the first time the troops under his command. Then there was trouble with the loading of the transports. These were not 'tactically' loaded for an opposed landing, and had to be re-stowed. Add to which, the emphasis on speed and the continually amended time-table were playing havoc with administration. And, to crown all, final agreement on a Menace plan was reached only on the 21st August.

But whatever the difficulties and complications, it was now

---

* Less than 20 ALC were available for his whole force along with 37 lifeboats and 15 motor boats.

too late for further changes. On the 27th August the War Cabinet considered the completed plans for Operation Menace and formally agreed to the go-ahead.[12] Despite the leakages and General Irwin's misgivings, they judged the operation justified in view of the objectives it was designed to achieve. If they still had doubts about it, there was encouragement in the news that Chad and the Cameroons had been won over to the Free French the day before.

This was glad tidings for de Gaulle as he prepared to leave London for embarkation at Liverpool. On the 16th August he had received a telegram from his associate Colonel Larminat, in Africa, of considerable import. Larminat strongly advised against a Dakar operation on account of the strength of the port's defences and the large forces needed to overcome them, and recommended action in the Cameroons instead.[13] De Gaulle had agreed to plans for small Free French forces to take Duala in the Cameroons and Fort Lamy in the Chad territory, but—brushing aside the warning about Dakar—had opposed delaying Operation Menace on any pretext. The Prime Minister and the Chiefs of Staff had concurred, and General Giffard, General Officer Commanding, West Africa, was asked to assist the Duala operation in every way possible. On the 26th the Governor of Chad territory declared for de Gaulle, on the next night Duala was won over, and on the 28th Brazzaville, capital of French Equatorial Africa, fell after two hours' fighting.

But now, along with the final agreement to launch Menace, there was a bitter last-minute dispute: over the matter of the Bamako gold. At Bamako in the French Sudan, the Bank of France had deposited a large store of gold for its own account and for the National Banks of Belgium and Poland. While the Belgians and Poles wanted to recover their share, Britain—without claiming ownership of the gold—wished to use it all to pay for purchase of war material from America. De Gaulle refused to entertain the British request, despite Spears' warning that the Government might abandon the expedition unless he consented. In the end the British gave in, accepting de Gaulle's proposal that only so much of the gold would be used as was needed to pay for British purchases on behalf of the Free French.

The die was cast. Operation Menace would sail on 31st August, and the 'strike' would be made on 19th September. Since its inception two months before, the plan for Dakar had been considered and re-considered, shaped and re-shaped, enlarged from a modest and purely French scheme into a major project involving powerful British support. Though toned down from the expansive concept outlined by Churchill in early August, the plan remained essentially the same: when the Anglo-French fleet arrived off Dakar, de Gaulle would send in emissaries with a message for the Governor, followed by his own troops, to take over the city peaceably for the Free French. This, as he had repeatedly stressed, should be a bloodless operation, accomplished by persuasion, hoped-for backing from within, and the impressive presence of the Anglo-French armada lying off-shore. If—as was thought unlikely—the Dakar garrison resisted, the Free French would use the minimum force necessary to overcome it. Only in the event of determined opposition would the British intervene. Then, as Churchill had said, they 'would use all means to break down resistance.' The whole operation was to be completed in one day, between dawn and dusk.

It was a bold and ambitious enterprise, but would it work? As an attempt to launch a combined land-and-sea operation it had nothing to go on except the abortive Norway expedition of the previous April. This move to counter the German occupation of the Norwegian ports had been a notable failure. The forces involved were mostly half-trained territorial units, unprepared to carry out a landing against opposition. The ability of the German air arm, holding as it did most of Norway's air fields, to hamper British operations had not been foreseen. Counsels were divided as to whether Narvik or Trondheim should be the principal objective. Conflicting orders to the commanders on the spot had been issued by the Admiralty and War Office. All this provided many lessons on how not to handle a combined operation. But if the planners could profit by the

Norway experience, in any case Dakar presented a very different problem from Norway. Tactical planning, organization, equipment and training for such an operation were all unknown factors.

Moreover, the operation was relying on an Anglo-French liaison and understanding that had been far from perfect. Its preparation, too, had been dogged by delays and its security possibly endangered. The Chiefs of Staff and General Irwin had not been happy about it for political or military reasons. And it depended for its success on the accuracy of encouraging reports about the support de Gaulle would find in Dakar, and about the comparative weakness of Dakar's defences. If these proved false and there were more than token resistance, calling for Anglo-French retaliation and thereby causing de Gaulle to abandon his 'no bloodshed' pledge, the whole operation might fail.

This was the picture on the 28th August, the day—72 hours from the convoy's sailing—that the Joint Commanders received their Final Directives for Operation Menace as approved by Churchill. It was not a brilliantly hopeful picture. But it was disastrously changed for the worse when late that same night the two liaison officers, Commander Rushbrooke and Captain Poulter, arrived back in London from Africa with their long-awaited report on the situation at Dakar. From this it was clear that Menace had virtually no chance of success.

Cunningham and Irwin were preparing to catch the night train to Liverpool when they learnt of the officers' arrival. Late as it was, they saw them immediately, and next day the officers were interviewed by the CIGS at the War Office. Their report was plainly a bombshell. In the cautious words of the official record of Operation Menace, 'they brought valuable information about the details and great strength of the defences, and they laid stress on the loyalty of the garrison to the commander, and of the commander and the Governor to Pétain. They were convinced that any attempt by General de Gaulle would be resolutely opposed. Captain Poulter, in particular, felt this

strongly.' Poulter indeed seems to have been embarrassingly
assertive. A footnote to the record adds: 'There is a conflict of
evidence as to the emphasis which Captain Poulter laid on the
loyalty of the garrison to Vichy. He maintains that his words,
in his interview with the Joint Commanders, were: "Not one
man, woman or child is pro-de Gaulle." The Joint Commanders
do not admit he was so emphatic.'[14]

Whatever Poulter actually said, the implications of his and
Rushbrooke's report were grave indeed. In plain terms, Operation Menace would never achieve its object and might as well
be cancelled. But could it be called off at this eleventh hour,
after all the planning and preparation, and in view of the hopes
that had been placed on it? For the War Office chiefs and the
Joint Commanders the dilemma was acute. But in the circumstances there could be only one decision: disregard the officers'
evidence and carry on with Menace. The footnote makes this
clear by adding that Poulter's 'testimony could hardly have
been accepted without abandoning the enterprise, and it was
inevitably overborne at this stage by the course of events.'[15]

For the Joint Commanders (as Irwin afterwards recalled)
the Dakar report was 'most discouraging.' 'However,' he added,
'it was too late to think of withdrawing, and no good thinking
all was lost at this stage. You may ask why we did not call it off
when we found out the real facts and while we still had the
chance to cancel the whole thing. I have no good answer to that
except that we didn't want to.'[16] What astonished the Commanders was the officers' estimate of the lack of support for de
Gaulle. Information coming from de Gaulle's own staff had
assessed 70% of the garrison as pro-de Gaulle, 20% neutral,
and only 10% pro-Vichy. These had been the best available
figures on which to base the strength of Dakar's opposition.
The only contrary assessment had come from Colonel Larminat
a fortnight before—and Larminat's chill warning about the
port's powerful defences seems for some extraordinary reason
to have been ignored. But now, on the eve of the expedition's
departure, no one responsible was in the mood to abandon
Menace. 'There was little time (and possibly little inclination),'

as Irwin's CSO I, Lt-Colonel Smith-Hill, put it, 'to examine in detail an opinion which, if accepted, would inevitably lead to a last-minute cancellation of the whole operation.'[17]

The irony of the matter was that the information that Rushbrooke and Poulter now brought should have been available to the Menace planners a good fortnight earlier. Ordered to return home on 10th August to provide much-needed intelligence about Dakar's defences, they had been delayed at Lagos by lack of planes. More ironic still, the officers had actually sent a plan of the French West Africa defence scheme to the War Office, but by some blunder (not the last in the story of Operation Menace) this had never been forwarded to the Joint Commanders or anyone else concerned.

And now, for the hapless Rushbrooke and Poulter, there was a shock in store. Having just landed in England, they found themselves bundled forthwith on to the flagship *Devonshire* to travel back to Africa, so that Cunningham and Irwin could examine them further on the Dakar situation during the voyage.

All in all, 'this doubtful and complex affair,' as Churchill called it, was going ahead with some strong cards stacked against it. A host of things could go wrong, but at that desperate phase of the war when there was little more to lose but everything to gain, it was seen as a gamble worth taking. And apart from its interest for Britain and de Gaulle, there was another powerful reason for staging Operation Menace. The future of Dakar was of vital concern to the United States. Since the start of the century it had been a key matter of American policy to oppose the presence of Germany as a transatlantic neighbour. The fall of France had greatly increased this risk, threatening to throw open to the Germans the French Atlantic ports of Casablanca and Dakar. German possession or use of Dakar, especially, could gravely imperil American security. From this nearest point to the American continent, a well-equipped military, naval and air base, Hitler's forces could menace America's air and sea communications and in the last resort launch an invasion of the United States. President Roosevelt and his Government were thus watching the Anglo-French plans to take over

Dakar with closest attention. When Churchill had consulted Roosevelt about the operation, the President was said to have replied: 'OK, but above all succeed!' Thus for Churchill, anxious to convince the President that Britain was worth supporting in her solitary fight against the Axis, Operation Menace—uncertain hazard though it was—became an enterprise that it was all the more essential to attempt, and bring off successfully.

CHAPTER III

CONVOY TO FREETOWN

Operation Menace was to sail in three sections, from Scapa, the Clyde and Liverpool. As finally assembled, it comprised six transports carrying some 2,700 Free French and 4,200 British troops, two Free French sloops, various storeships and Admiral Cunningham's Force M (the naval force detailed for the operation): the battleship *Barham*, the cruisers *Devonshire* and *Fiji* and seven destroyers. Force M was to be joined en route by the battleship *Resolution*, the aircraft carrier *Ark Royal*, and a number of destroyers, seconded to Cunningham from Admiral Somerville's Force H based at Gibraltar. Before proceeding to Dakar the whole armada would call at the British port of Freetown, in Sierra Leone, for re-fuelling and re-grouping.

In its modest way, the operation was making history. For the first time since the disasters of Dunkirk and the fall of France, the Allies were hitting back with a combined 'offensive' launched from British shores. Even as the invasion threat was reaching its climax, with massed barges on the French coast and air attacks on Britain that were beginning to strain the defences to their limits, an Anglo-French strike force was taking the initiative. All this was heartening. But as if to foreshadow the mishaps and set-backs that would later overtake Menace, at several points the pre-embarkation moves got off to a slightly farcical start.

At Euston station, on 30th August, the crowded special train scheduled to take de Gaulle, most of the Spears Mission and various French and British officers to Liverpool, was held up by the non-appearance of the officer who was bringing the funds needed for the expedition. Finally he arrived, hurrying up the platform alongside a truck bearing 50,000 dollars in cash and escorted by a single guard. He had been delayed at the War Office because the staff there had gone to ground during an air raid, and he had had 'to practically shoot his way out.'[1] That was not all. The train started, jerked to a halt and then backed and stopped to await a trolley stacked with bales of papers being trundled towards the guard's van. As these were being loaded on to the van one burst open, to scatter over the platform, for everyone to see, a shower of leaflets boldly headlined: 'Aux Citoyens de Dakar.'

By an unhappy coincidence the same thing happened at two other places. Petty Officer T. T. Jenkins of H.M.S. *Devonshire*, anchored on the Clyde, vividly recalls seeing bales of similar leaflets bursting open on the dockside at Greenock.[2] And on the evidence of Evelyn Waugh, in charge of troops embarking earlier at Liverpool before sailing north for training to Scapa, a carelessly dropped package marked 'Most Secret' broke apart to release hundreds of blue, white and red sheets bearing the slogan: 'Français de Dakar! Joignez-vous à nous pour délivrer la France! Général de Gaulle.' To advertise the expedition still further, a broken crate on Liverpool's quayside spewed out a shower of de Gaulle souvenir medals, which were eagerly pocketed by the dockers.

Most of the British troops had no idea where they were going. They had arrived at Liverpool, issued with tropical kit including unwieldy pith helmets, vaguely under the impression that they were bound for the Middle East, Ceylon or Malaya. The confusion that marked the general embarkation proceedings at Liverpool was increased by the heavy bombing the port was then undergoing. The ships and quays were shrouded in a total blackout. As the bombs fell, embarkation officers who had been inspecting their lists with dimmed torches took cover until the all-clear sounded. For those sailing earlier to Scapa or leaving direct from Liverpool, it was an inauspicious send-off.

The Liverpool convoy—consisting of the British transport *Karanja*, carrying the 5th Battalion, 101st Royal Marines Brigade; the 16,000-ton Dutch liner *Westernland*, carrying de Gaulle and his staff, most of the Spears Mission and 1,200 Free French troops; the Dutch liner *Pennland*, carrying an 1,100-strong Free French contingent under the command of Lt-Colonel Magrin-Vernerey; and the small cargo boat *Belgravia*, loaded with provisions for the people of Dakar—left Liverpool on the 31st August, escorted by three destroyers.

The Scapa convoy—comprising the transports *Ettrick*, *Kenya* and *Sobieski*, with the 1st, 2nd and 3rd Battalions, 101st R.M. Brigade commanded by Brigadier St Clair Morford, and ancillary and Free French liaison troops—left the same day, escorted by the cruiser *Fiji* and three destroyers.

The Clyde group—Force M's flagship, the 8-inch-gun cruiser *Devonshire* (Captain J. M. Mansfield, D.S.O.) and one destroyer, along with the two Free French sloops *Commandant Duboc* and *Commandant Dominé*—left on the 31st August to join the Liverpool convoy on 1st September at a point to the north of Ireland. Sailing on the flagship with Cunningham were General Irwin and his staff.

The Clyde and Liverpool groups were to rendezvous next day with the Scapa convoy and proceed south at 12 knots, forming the convoy MP. Meanwhile the destroyers would return to Scapa. The rest of Cunningham's Force M—the battleship *Barham* (Captain G. C. Cooke) and four destroyers—had left Scapa on the 28th August for Gibraltar, where it would pick up the ships attached to it from the Gibraltar-based Force H (the battleship *Resolution* commanded by Captain O. Bevir), the aircraft carrier *Ark Royal* commanded by Captain C. S. Holland, and six destroyers, and proceed with them to join the convoy en route to its intermediate destination, Freetown.

The half-dozen vessels of the Liverpool convoy steamed out into the Atlantic, zigzagging to avoid U-boats. Now the enterprise had started, de Gaulle stood on the deck of the *Western-land* and pondered on his situation. As he later confessed, he was feeling 'crushed by the dimensions of duty.' He saw the blacked-out, unarmed foreign ship in which he sailed as carrying 'the fortunes of France.'[3] Spears on the other hand felt reassured and hopeful. He had the impression that 'the whole thing was beginning to shake down.'[4] But there was still much planning to do, and at once the Mission members settled in to a round of conferences. They also had to study the briefing material they had brought with them—the handbooks on West Africa, latest intelligence reports on Dakar, meteorological data for Dakar at this season (data which, it was noted, virtually guaranteed clear skies and fine settled weather).

De Gaulle and Spears had their own corner of the ship, a roped-off part of one deck where they could talk in privacy. De Gaulle himself liked to spend long hours poring over a large-scale map of Africa. Otherwise he forgathered, amicably enough, with the French and British staffs in the mess. Soon the first rather grim mood pervading the *Westernland* relaxed and there was an almost carefree spirit aboard. But for the British this was roughly dispelled by radio reports of the heavy bombing of London on 7th September, the day when Goering's air force launched their first great attack on the capital. As the raids continued, their worry was increased by lack of news about the extent of casualties and damage. They were however cheered by the figures announced of German losses. De Gaulle, who had been following the reports closely, shared the general optimism. 'They cannot keep this up,' he reassured Spears. 'You have won.'

Every deck of the *Westernland* was packed with Free French troops: Foreign Legion men and many North Africans. As the convoy steamed southwards the heat below decks, with the enforced black-out and the few electric fans on board reserved for the sick bay, grew intense and discipline on the ship became strained. There were frequent knife fights, and once in the black-out Spears stumbled over a corpse outside his cabin. The tough ship's captain, Piet Langeay, clamped down heavily on disorder, quelling the beginnings of a stokers' mutiny by locking up the ringleaders in the *Westernland*'s deepest hold. Added to the general discomfort was the ever-present threat of U-boat attack. To minimize the threat the convoy had been routed by way of the Azores before heading for the African coast. But already there had been one casualty. When one day out from Scapa, the escort cruiser *Fiji* was damaged by a torpedo and forced to return to port. Its place was taken by the cruiser *Australia*, hurriedly dispatched from the Home Fleet.

Thrown so closely into de Gaulle's company on the *Westernland*, Spears was learning much about this man who was taking on himself the leadership of the Free French. Now he jotted in his diary: 'There is much timidity in him, overcome by will: he doesn't show timidity when doing his job or dealing with subordinates.' But having previously remarked on de Gaulle's willingness to listen to his advice, Spears was now taken aback by his brusque refusal to consider a suggestion made by him on some minor affair. 'So you don't like having suggestions made?' asked Spears, somewhat nettled. 'No,' replied de Gaulle tartly. 'On purely personal matters, I like doing things my way.'[5]

One thing de Gaulle was adamant about. He was determined at all costs to keep his autonomy of command. 'On 10th September, Cunningham and Irwin signalled him from the flagship *Devonshire* proposing that he should exercise his command of the Free French from their ship. Backed by Spears, de Gaulle declined. In his reply he gave four reasons for staying on the *Westernland*: his chances of success would be greatly diminished if the Free French operation were directed from a British ship; he would not wish to direct a purely French operation from a British ship; a successful Free French operation directed from a British ship would have unfavourable later repercussions; de Gaulle did not wish to be on a British ship in case of 'Nasty' (the eventuality that demanded a full-scale British attack, including a landing by British troops). To have been on a British ship during shelling would not only be distasteful, but would have impossible repercussions on the eventual operation.[6] As later events were to show, de Gaulle's decision was a grave error. In thus isolating himself from the Joint Commanders—in what was in effect the Combined Operations Ship—he was hampering efficient consultation and rapid decision-making and generally jeopardizing the co-operation of command that might well be vital for the success of Menace.

On the flagship *Devonshire* General Irwin was immersed in work and feverishly trying to make up for lost time. He now had to do all the detailed planning that had been impossible to start before sailing. Fortunately Captain Poulter, sailing on the flagship, had with him a copy of the French West Africa Defence Plan, and this Irwin spent the first two days at sea in intensively studying. The ludicrously outdated information about Dakar that the Joint Commanders had had to rely on in London was shown from the statement in it that the construction of a General Post Office, schools and various new buildings was projected for 1919! Now they learned with a shock that the forces at Dakar included a mobile infantry brigade, a Senegalese brigade, together with garrison companies. And the artillery in the coastal forts comprised eight 9.4-in guns, 25 5.4-in guns and 18 3- or 4-in guns. This may have helped convince the Menace staff who, in the words of Captain Walter, had tended to mistrust Poulter's 'tales of woe.'

Irwin's small staff—a GSO I, GSO II, GSO III, AA and QMG officers, two Intelligence officers (one of whom was Poulter), a Signals officer and three clerks—was toiling night and day to produce the massive detailed orders that would be needed in the event of an opposed landing. No conference with subordinate officers was possible until arrival at Freetown (and there the stay would be only brief), so everything had now to be typed out specifying the necessary action right down to unit level. The clerks were inexperienced and typed slowly, with many mistakes. The Military Operational Orders ran to 80 pages, and the Intelligence, Signals Instructions and General Instructions to 60 pages. 205 copies had to be produced—a total of over 28,000 sheets. This gargantuan task was tackled with two typewriters, one of which was faulty, and a duplicator that often broke down. In addition the duplicating paper ran out and the stationery supplied by the War Office lacked file covers, paper clips and ink pots. The 'office' was a cabin seven feet square; and in this minuscule nerve-centre the heat, with the temperature soaring to 90 degrees, became purgatorial. As the *Devonshire* ploughed southwards, Irwin's exhausted staff laboured on, in what Smith-Hill described as 'an infernal sweating twilight.' For Irwin a further difficulty was communication. Because of the need for wireless silence, all communication with his subordinate commanders was by lamp. This meant that he had to inform Brigadier St Clair Morford, the Marine commander in charge of the landing operation, of the progress of the planning by sporadic flashings from the *Devonshire* to the *Ettrick*.

Very different were conditions on the transports. Aboard the *Karanja*, a converted P. & O. liner, something of a holiday atmosphere prevailed. For the officers there was comfort and even luxury reminiscent of peacetime. Deferential Goanese stewards were at their beck and call, waking them with tea and orange juice, summoning them to meals with tinkling oriental xylophone music. Cigarettes and gin were duty-free. And, in the words of Captain Mitchell, a member of the Spears Mission who would later join Spears on the *Westernland*, 'meals excellent, no stint of tea, sugar or butter, partridge, grouse and all manner of fish.'[7] But despite the mishaps at Euston and on the Liverpool dockside which had blazoned the name of Dakar, aboard the *Karanja* there was some uncertainty about the convoy's destination even as late as sailing-time. Mitchell knew for sure that they were going to Dakar only when a colleague, Major Wingate, told him at sea a day after sailing.

In Mitchell's case, secrecy about Operation Menace had been carried to almost extreme lengths. He had been appointed to the Spears Mission in August, after it had been ascertained that he could speak French and was willing to serve with the Free French forces. Having obtained a revolver, binoculars and a French–English dictionary of military terms, he was injected for yellow fever and briefed on the arms and equipment used by the Free French. He was then told the Mission would be leaving England soon, but not informed where it was going. A talk by General Spears to Mission members followed, but still with no hint of destination. An interview with a War Office general three days before sailing was equally uninformative. Mitchell learnt most from the tailor supplying his tropical kit, who told him the name of the ship he would travel on, and the date of sailing.

Major Ronald Wingate, of the Indian Political Service, another member of the Spears Mission, was luckier. After being hurriedly commissioned and attached to the Mission in August, he was briefed by Spears and told that his particular role with the Mission would be to help in organizing essential supplies in and out of French West Africa. Either then or very soon after, he was informed about Dakar, being impressed with the vital need for secrecy. Just before sailing he was given three days to collect a ship-load of condensed milk, flour and other provisions intended for distribution to the people of Dakar. Now, as the convoy breasted the Atlantic waves, the small ship carrying this cargo, the *Belgravia*, trailed behind the *Karanja*. Pointing the *Belgravia* out to Mitchell, Wingate told him how he had had to cut through the toils of red tape to get the stores.

Along with its Royal Marines battalion, the *Karanja* carried a party of six officers and 30 men of various units in Mitchell's charge. For the Marines there was continued preparation and briefing for the landing they would have to execute if de Gaulle's 'friendly' approach at Dakar failed. 'Lecture by the Marine colonel to his officers on the forthcoming landing,' Mitchell recorded on the 4th September. 'Sketch on a blackboard. Their task to land on the beach through surf, mount a cliff 100 feet high and hold the main streets against the rushing up of reinforcements while others raking the forts. This will be preceded by a naval bombardment.' At another lecture on the 6th, 'the officers say they would let French civilians through in the middle of an operation if they wanted to go to their homes. Wingate rises and forcibly explodes this fallacy.'[8]

On the transport *Ettrick*, out from Scapa, mild chaos had

reigned as it had earlier left Liverpool to sail north to its Scapa training area. There had been a hasty re-shuffle of troops when it was discovered that some units had been wrongly embarked on it. And then, on the point of sailing, the *Ettrick* had had to return to the quayside for the cargo to be reloaded in 'tactical order' after the ammunition was found stowed beneath piles of beer crates and NAAFI stores. The *Ettrick*, like the *Karanja*, was a converted P. & O. liner. Besides its Marines contingent, it carried Free French liaison officers, a naval beach-party, some chaplains and various assorted personnel.

The officers' living conditions were as lavish as those on the *Karanja*. First-class accommodation, early morning tea served by smiling Goanese stewards, five-course meals announced by musical gong-sounding, and bargain-price drink, gave this military operation, in the words of one officer, the air of 'a hilarious luxury cruise.' Daily news bulletins were broadcast over the ship's loudspeaker, interspersed with music from Ivor Novello records. As on the other transports, the euphoric holiday atmosphere was damped by the announcement of the first big raids on London. But even the torpedoing of the *Fiji* 'was soon forgotten,' notes the officer, 'in yet another round of John Collinses.'[9]

Only slightly less comfortable were the senior NCO's in the tourist class. But in sharp contrast were the conditions for the other ranks. Crowded on to converted messdecks, at night they sweated in their close-slung hammocks under battened hatches. Their daytime routine was not demanding. They were kept in trim with PT and boxing, and given lectures on Dakar, General de Gaulle, malaria, and, in the words of Evelyn Waugh, an officer on the *Ettrick*, 'the importance of keeping clear of native women.' Otherwise they lazed about on the forward deck and in the evenings attended concerts organized by the chaplains. So far, this was indeed the war's strangest operation. Aboard the *Ettrick*, as on the other British transports, there was no mood of stern anticipation, no feeling that the troops might be going into battle. Instead, a half-humorous, rather bewildered speculation as to what the expedition was all about. Even officers found it hard to take things seriously. What Lt Palmer, sailing in the *Ettrick*, now chiefly recalls about his briefing for the 'attack' is that he was to land with his men at the Sultan's Bathing Hut.

So, in idyllic conditions, the convoy sailed on through calm blue seas, two groups of three transports, each in line astern. Fussing alongside them were the two French sloops, and ahead steamed the flagship *Devonshire*. On the 6th September the small armada had passed the Azores, on the 10th it was abreast of Africa's Rio de Oro, on the 12th it made contact with planes from the aircraft-carrier *Ark Royal*, leading the combined force from Gibraltar. There were no more U-boat alarms. In the bright sunshine and balmy air it seemed more than ever like a holiday cruise. 'Hard to realize this is a warlike expedition,' noted Spears on the *Westernland*.[10] Then suddenly, on Friday 13th September, came news that changed everything. At 5 pm Spears picked up an Empire broadcast from London that six French warships had passed through the Straits of Gibraltar and were at large in the Atlantic.

CHAPTER IV

ENTER THE VICHY CRUISERS

This was startling news. It posed the ominous questions: did Vichy know about Operation Menace and were the warships heading to attack the convoy or reinforce Dakar's defences? If so, and in view of the poor security prevailing during Menace's preparation Vichy might well have got wind of it, the operation seemed doomed to failure or at least gravely threatened. In any case it was difficult to think that the Vichy warships had nothing to do with the Allied attempt on Dakar: no such vessels had gone through the Straits since the fall of France the previous June. That in itself raised another question: how had they got past Gibraltar? As yet the ships were hundreds of miles away to the north-east, but southward-bound on a course that could bring them to Dakar. For the Menace chiefs it was at the moment all speculation, though with very unpleasant possibilities. But the appearance on the scene of the Vichy ships was one of those strange twists that were to mark the whole story of Operation Menace. What the commanders could not know was that the warships were unaware of the existence of the Menace convoy and on a mission totally unconnected with Dakar.

Even more odd, at this stage the French leaders knew nothing of Operation Menace. The first news of de Gaulle's departure from England had reached Vichy on 8th September, when he had already been at sea for a week. The report had been passed to the Spanish Government by Spain's Ambassador in London, the Duke d'Alba, and transmitted from Madrid to the Spanish Ambassador to Vichy, Señor Lequérica. Lequérica immediately informed Paul Baudouin, Vichy's Foreign Minister, but gave Morocco as de Gaulle's probable destination, the inference being that the Free French leader was aiming to rally resistance in North Africa.

Baudouin was worried less by the threat of de Gaulle's landing in North Africa than by the possibility that the Germans would use the threat as a pretext for occupying North Africa themselves. This he regarded as a catastrophe to be avoided at all costs. He therefore conceived the idea of sending a strongly-worded telegram to General Noguès, North Africa's Commander-in-Chief, ordering him to arrest de Gaulle on his arrival and treat him as an 'outlaw'. The real purpose of the telegram was to demonstrate to the Germans that the French were determined to deal with de Gaulle themselves, without German intervention. Baudouin at once reported to Marshal Pétain and explained his plan. The Marshal approved and the cable went off to General Noguès at Rabat. To make sure the Germans would know about it Baudouin arranged with General Huntziger to telephone it at once to the German Armistice Commission headquarters at Wiesbaden. Next day Baudouin's *chef de cabinet* flew to Rabat to put Noguès in the picture.

The ploy was part of a continuous policy on the part of Vichy rather than an isolated move. Vichy had been concerned about possible German intervention in Africa for some time. The recent Free French successes in Equatorial Africa had intensified this concern. Hitler, it was feared, might decide to pre-empt further Gaullist landings by sending German troops to occupy key African points. The best way to prevent this was for Vichy to convince the Germans it could itself defend French African territory. If the actual use of force was ruled out, there could at least be a show of force sufficient to stop further secessions to de Gaulle. It was for this mission that—four days before the sailing of the Dakar expedition and with Vichy unaware even of its existence—the French warships were called into action.

On the 27th August Admiral Bourrague, commanding the

45

4th Cruiser Division at Toulon, was ordered to assemble a group comprising the three cruisers of his division and the three destroyers of the 10th Division. Next day he was called to Vichy by Darlan, Minister of Marine, and directed to put his ships on a war footing. Besides his flagship the *Georges Leygues* the group included the cruisers *Montcalm* and *Gloire* and the destroyers *Fantasque*, *Audacieux* and *Malin*. On the 30th the group was designated Force Y and its destination, Pointe Noire, in French Equatorial Africa, announced. Brief calls for re-fuelling were to be made at Casablanca and Dakar. If poor security endangered the success of Operation Menace, it certainly threatened Bourrague's mission. The quays of Toulon buzzed with talk about the operation, providing a field-day for any sharp-eared Free French agent who happened to be there. But, as with Operation Menace, on all the evidence no news of it leaked to the other side. So, ironically, these two almost simultaneous expeditions proceeded without the adversaries knowing about them.

On the 3rd September Force Y received its general orders. Two days later these were amplified, specifying a naval operation at Pointe Noire for the 15th, and emphasizing that Force Y's main role was to ensure that the French colonies remained under the regime of the Vichy Government. An important instruction issued by the joint German and Italian Armistice Commission, which was responsible for authorizing the operation, directed that Bourrague's squadron should defend itself in the case of British attack and under no circumstances allow any of his vessels to fall into British hands. Armed with these orders the six warships of Force Y sailed from Toulon at 4 pm on the 9th. Full speed of 25 knots was to be maintained, to allow for reaching the Straits of Gibraltar at dawn on the 11th. In accordance with the French Admiralty's practice, the British authorities were to be informed forthwith.

The scene shifts to Gibraltar, headquarters of Admiral Sir Dudley North, Commander-in-Chief, North Atlantic station.

On the evening of 9th September Admiral North had just sat

1. General Spears and General de Gaulle on board s.s. *Westernland*

2. General Spears, General de Gaulle and General Irwin in conference on the bridge of s.s. *Westernland*

3. General N. M. S. Irwin, Joint Commander of the Dakar expedition

down to dinner at his residence, the Mount, with his colleague, Vice-Admiral Sir James Somerville, when his Flag Lieutenant handed him a signal marked 'Immediate' from the British Consul in Tangier. It ran: 'French squadron may try to pass Straits proceeding westwards unknown destination. Attempt may be timed to take place in next 72 hours.'

North checked that the signal had been sent on to London and, amid the buzz of speculation that ran round the table, hazarded the guess that the ships might be making for Casablanca to escape the Germans. In any case there was no undue worry, for the latest Admiralty orders, as North interpreted them, left the decision as to intercepting Vichy French warships with the Admiralty itself. Any action by him now therefore depended on orders received from London, following the receipt there of the Tangier signal.

Admiralty orders on the handling of French warships were in fact somewhat unclear. Since the Mers-el-Kebir episode in early July there had been a string of instructions, not always consistent. Immediately after Mers-el-Kebir the Admiralty had directed that the Navy was to be prepared for attack but was not to fire the first shot. Then had come other orders seeming to modify this and leaving North in doubt as to what action he should take against Vichy warships attempting to pass through the Straits. On asking the Admiralty for clarification he had been told that contact with equal or superior forces should be avoided, but that inferior forces should be stopped and ordered into port. But another order had quickly followed, directing that no further action should be taken against French ships in their colonial and North African ports. This seemed to North to cancel the previous interception order. He therefore judged that no action should be taken by him against ships in or proceeding to such ports as Casablanca or Dakar, unless on specific Admiralty orders.[1]

Neither North's nor Somerville's forces at Gibraltar could have been very effective against a strong flotilla just then. North had nine ancient destroyers and a few minesweepers. Somerville, commanding the mobile Force H, had only the battlecruiser

Renown and four destroyers—the rest of his force having left on the 6th to strengthen Admiral Cunningham's Force M. And, in the event of joint action being necessary, the command situation would have presented slight problems. For Somerville, though junior to North, was independent of him and controlled direct by the Admiralty.

By midnight on the 9th, Gibraltar's Naval Operations Room had heard nothing from London on the Tangier signal: it was probably too early for a reply. Meanwhile, a few hundred miles to the north-east, the French squadron, out from Toulon, was maintaining a steady 25 knots towards the Straits. Bourrague was making no secret of his movements. As the squadron sailed on over the flat Mediterranean, every ship shone its deck and navigation lights. And they were ordered to give their names if challenged.

Next morning there was still no signal from the Admiralty. And nothing came through all day. North and Somerville were puzzled that their Lordships were taking so long to react. Though they had no reason to think they would have to take action, they would have appreciated some confirmatory guidance or instructions—some acknowledgement at any rate. As it happened, the lack of secrecy about the flotilla's movements was endorsed that day by Admiral Darlan himself, who signalled his Naval Attaché in Madrid: 'You are to inform the British that Admiral Bourrague will be passing Gibraltar at 0845 on September 11.' As a result, late that evening the British Ambassador in Madrid, Sir Samuel Hoare, was informed by the Spanish Foreign Minister, Colonel Beigbeder, of the forthcoming passage of the ships through the Straits.

Hoare immediately passed the information to London. At the same time the Naval Attaché, Madrid, signalled Gibraltar: 'French Admiralty's to me begins—Please advise naval authorities at Gibraltar departure from Toulon September 9 three cruisers type *George Leygues* and three destroyers *Fantasque* class which will pass Straits a.m. September 11.' About midnight on the 10th, North's Chief of Staff passed this to the admiral. North—still with no word from the Admiralty—

quickly ordered a destroyer-group headed by the *Hotspur*, which was out submarine-hunting east of the Straits, to report at once if the flotilla was sighted. Some hours later the *Hotspur* reported a spotting and signalled: 'Am shadowing.' Meanwhile, at 5.30 am on the 11th the Force H commander, Admiral Somerville, who had been kept informed of the situation, ordered the *Renown* to an hour's steam to intercept the Vichy ships.

By 7 am North, in mounting exasperation, had flashed the Admiralty two 'Immediate' signals. The second read: 'Intend to keep in touch with the force by air and will report probable destination.' But from the Admiralty in London, still silence. Then, at 8.40, in the sharp early sunlight, the six Vichy warships streaked westwards past the Rock. In passing, each ship winked out its name. North could do no more. He told his Chief of Staff to make them a signal. 'Something like "Bon Voyage",' he said. Then he rang Somerville in the *Renown*. Somerville agreed that the Admiralty did not want them to do anything: otherwise they would have signalled by then. General Sir Clive Liddell, the Governor of Gibraltar, also concurred that there was nothing North could do without fresh orders.

An hour later Somerville decided to drop the *Renown* back to two hours' steam, and rang North to get his agreement. North was emphatic that London would have informed them if there had been any change in policy respecting British action against Vichy naval forces. What had astonished the two admirals more than anything in the thirty-six hours since they had received the Tangier signal was the profound and utter silence of the Admiralty. Now at last the silence was to be broken. At 1 pm, just as Somerville was going to lunch he received an Admiralty signal (dispatch-time 12.40) ordering the *Renown* and all available destroyers to raise steam for full speed. An hour later he received another: 'Proceed to sea and endeavour obtain contact French force.'

At 4.30 pm the *Renown*, with accompanying destroyers, steamed out of harbour—to start a chase that was already doomed. At that moment Bourrague's force was putting into

Casablanca. Minutes later North himself received another Admiralty signal: 'Three French cruisers type *Georges Leygues* and three cruisers *Fantasque* class approaching Gibraltar from east at 0515/9/11.' It had gone out at 3 o'clock (over six hours after the ships had *passed* the Rock). Reading it, Admiral North allowed himself a quiet—and in the circumstances remarkably mild—exclamation: 'It's fantastic!'

Fantastic it certainly was. As the Dakar convoy sailed all unsuspecting towards Africa, somewhere along the line between Gibraltar and the Admiralty in London a massive failure in command or communications had occurred, with possibly fatal results for Operation Menace. The precise objective of the Atlantic-bound Vichy squadron was unknown to the British, both on the Rock and in London. There was small reason for North or Somerville to connect its movements with the Dakar operation, for though they knew that part of Somerville's Force H had just joined Cunningham's Force M, they knew little about Operation Menace itself. 'The Admiral was *not* in the Dakar circle,' as Churchill was later to emphasize about North.[2] In any case, fully familiar with standing Admiralty instructions about Vichy warships and aware that the Admiralty had been informed about the passage of Bourrague's squadron, they were only too anxious to hear from the Admiralty in case of any change of orders.

What Admirals North and Somerville could not guess, as they tensely awaited word from the Admiralty for 36 vital hours on the 10th and 11th September, was that there had been a monumental slip-up in Whitehall. The Madrid signal, sent to London on the evening of the 10th, and received before midnight, had not reached the Admiralty War Room until 9 am on the 11th. And the Tangier signal, addressed to the Foreign Office late on the 9th and received there at 7.50 am on the 10th, lay for several days undeciphered in a Foreign Office 'In' tray, to reach the First Sea Lord's desk only on the morning of the 13th.

For these astounding delays there were various reasons. The Madrid signal, though promptly deciphered and passed on, was held up by the Director of Operations Division (Foreign), who failed to assess its importance despite his being informed of the Dakar expedition. The Tangier signal, with its 24-hour start on the Madrid signal, became bogged-down in a pile of arrears in the Foreign Office cipher branch—the result of the constant stoppages of work due to the air raids then assailing London. But it was on neither of these signals that Admiral Sir Dudley Pound, the First Sea Lord, acted. The signal that alerted him was that from the destroyer *Hotspur* to North (and repeated to the Admiralty) timed around 5 am on the 11th, reporting the sighting of the Vichy squadron. Pound immediately perceived the possible threat to Dakar. And the Admiralty signal that Somerville received at about 2 pm that day, ordering him to proceed to sea, specified that he must prevent the French ships from reaching Dakar or any Biscay port, but might allow them to proceed to Casablanca. So belated was this order that had the squadron in fact been bound direct for Dakar, instead of Casablanca, it would have been impossible for him to stop them.

Two more signals of interest passed that day, the 11th. One was from the Admiralty to Somerville, leading Force H in the *Renown* somewhere at sea between Gibraltar and Casablanca. It ordered him that evening to set up a patrol to intercept the Vichy ships if they moved south from Casablanca. Accordingly, until the 13th he was to patrol with the *Renown* and five destroyers between Cape Blanco and Agadir. But Somerville was unlucky. During the 12th and 13th Casablanca was obscured by haze and a British reconnaissance plane flying over the harbour was shot down. Consequently reports about the presence of additional warships were inconclusive, and by the time Somerville received an air reconnaissance report at 4.20 pm on the 13th that there were no cruisers at Casablanca, Bourrague's force had already sneaked out of harbour some 36 hours before and was making full speed for Dakar.

The other signal was from North to Cunningham, leading the Menace force somewhere at sea well south of the Azores, en route for Freetown. At about 1.15 pm on the 11th North signalled Cunningham informing him of the passage of the Vichy squadron through the Straits.[3] Cunningham therefore knew of this—without informing de Gaulle on the *Westernland*—a full two days before de Gaulle himself had learnt it from the BBC broadcast. His reason for not telling him immediately is not clear; but in this Anglo-French operation where close liaison might be vital for success the omission was peculiar, to say the least.

On the *Westernland*, the news about the Vichy ships had struck Spears and de Gaulle with consternation. For de Gaulle the report was a 'terrible blow', as Spears noted. Since leaving England he had been without any information about West Africa or Dakar. (It is uncertain whether he was told of the Rushbrooke-Poulter report, received just before sailing.) Anxious as he was for further news, he was prevented by the convoy's wireless silence from communicating with England. And with the radio bulletins from London confined mostly to reports of the Luftwaffe attacks on the capital, he was feeling increasingly cut off from vital news. Even contact with Cunningham on the *Devonshire* was limited to Morse signalling by lamp. Now the sudden terse announcement about the appearance of the French squadron had left him with a sense of impotence.

Spears' and de Gaulle's first obvious reaction was that Vichy knew of their plans and was attempting to stop them, perhaps under German orders. Or possibly that this was a general move by Pétain to counter the Free French threat to the African colonies. At once they signalled Cunningham on the *Devonshire* asking that a plane be sent to Freetown to check the report. Cunningham replied that the news was true (he had known this for two days) and that the six ships had called at Casablanca, possibly southward bound. De Gaulle and Spears then proposed that they should come over to the *Devonshire* for a conference. No, said Cunningham, he was short of water and could not delay. He would see them on the *Westernland* immediately on reaching Freetown. In growing impatience de Gaulle signalled back that everything possible must be done to stop the Vichy ships from reaching Dakar or any other West Africa port. If they reached Dakar it was most unlikely that they would surrender to him. He urged that a squadron accompanied by his sloop, the *Savorgnan de Brazza*, should intercept them. The *Savorgnan* would carry a letter from him directing them to place themselves under his orders and turn back to Casablanca, or take the consequences.[4]

Cunningham was as worried as de Gaulle. That evening he learnt that the French cruisers had sailed out of Casablanca, southward bound. Soon after, he received an Admiralty order to send all his available ships north to stop the cruisers entering Dakar. He therefore decided to see de Gaulle at once instead of waiting for arrival at Freetown. Just after midnight on the 13th he boarded the *Westernland*, accompanied by General Irwin. For de Gaulle and Spears this was none too soon. The Spears Mission's War Diary lamented 'that so many hours had been lost since they had first drawn Cunningham's attention to the importance of this situation. Cunningham's hands were tied to some extent by the fact that wireless silence was being observed, and so he could not obtain Admiralty instructions before they themselves initiated them. As it was, it was a question of minutes as to whether Cunningham could intercept the French cruisers before their arrival at Dakar.'[5]

Now, sweating in an airless, dim-lit cabin, glasses of tepid whisky beside them, the four men tensely discussed the position. 'De Gaulle's and my first idea,' Spears noted, 'was that Cunningham should have a French ship [to lead his interception force]. Only one any good was *Savorgnan de Brazza*, but he said it was too slow; this was a 25-knot job. He could only collect three cruisers, so all idea of an overwhelming force gone. The capital ships had to go on to get water. Can hardly imagine the French ships taking his orders. Desperate. Had a brain wave. Send d'Argenlieu with de Gaulle's letter? It is just possible he might get a word in—a French voice better than nothing.'[6] This was agreed. The British commanders left, along with d'Argenlieu, who bore de Gaulle's ultimatum. By 2.30 am on the 14th the flagship *Devonshire* and accompanying destroyers were steaming north towards Dakar, 400 miles off. For General Irwin, on the *Devonshire*, still wrestling with the mountainous task of preparing the operational orders, it was a frustrating moment. There was no time for him and his staff to be transferred from the flagship. And now he was being wafted away into the blue, to be totally isolated from his troops on the British transports. Other ships of Cunningham's force (the Gibraltar element) were hurrying to join him, reinforced by two cruisers, the *Cumberland* and *Cornwall*, seconded to him from the South Atlantic Fleet. On the *Westernland*, de Gaulle gave vent to the sardonic comment: '*le vendredi 13 est une date toujours à redouter* (Friday the 13th is always a date to be afraid of).'

Meanwhile the plans of the Vichy squadron had also suffered a change. After passing Gibraltar on the morning of the 11th, it had dropped anchor at Casablanca late that afternoon. Bourrague had intended to sail on next afternoon after refuelling. But a report around 8 pm from the Naval Commander in Morocco, Admiral d'Harcourt, brought him disquieting news. A large warship or aircraft-carrier had been spotted shortly before from Cape Spartel, in Tangier, moving south-west. Bourrague realised that the British were on his track (the ship was in fact Admiral Somerville's flagship *Renown*, from Gibraltar) and feared that if they made contact with him his squadron might suffer a similar fate to that of the French fleet at Mers-el-Kebir. He therefore decided to cancel his plans for an overnight stay and head on south immediately. Men on shore leave were recalled, refuelling was expedited and the squadron steamed out of port in the small hours of the 12th. The move was so hurried that some of the crew and a quantity of fresh provisions for Dakar were left behind.

It was soon obvious that the route was being watched. Just after leaving port the *Malin* was chased by what appeared to be a light cruiser and only escaped by putting on speed. And shortly before dawn the French submarine *Amphitrite* spotted one of Somerville's patrolling destroyers some 30 miles west of Casablanca. Then around 8 am, 60 miles west of Cap Martin, the *Renown* and several destroyers were seen, but Bourrague evaded observation by rounding the cape close inshore. The French admiral now decided that his only hope of reaching Dakar was to put on maximum speed and make a dash for it. His force put on every ounce of steam, streaking at 27 knots for Dakar. With no further incident the squadron reached Dakar at noon on the 14th. It had completely out-witted Admiral Somerville's patrol from Gibraltar, which had failed to stop its breakout from Casablanca over 48 hours before and remained on fruitless watch of the port until the previous afternoon.

Through the early hours of the 14th and most of that day, Cunningham's force steamed north on its new mission to stop the Vichy squadron reaching Dakar. D'Argenlieu, on board the *Devonshire* as the bearer of de Gaulle's ultimatum to Admiral Bourrague, found the British admiral 'somewhat annoyed by the affair.' Taciturn and lost in his thoughts, he only opened his mouth to speak of 'my old *Montcalm*', which had been under his orders the previous April during the Norway expedition'.[7] He was making no secret of his impatience at having to go back on his tracks and spread out his force over miles of ocean in this impromptu interception attempt. If he had believed in the sound sense of Operation Menace from the start, it was difficult not to feel that with the unforeseen intervention of Bourrague's warships the prospects of success were gravely diminished.

By early evening Cunningham's ships had established their patrol off Dakar. But they were too late by a matter of hours. The observer of a Skua plane from the aircraft carrier *Ark Royal*, flying over the port before nightfall, thought he spotted Bourrague's squadron but could not be sure. Next morning the French cruisers' presence was confirmed by two more Skuas which clearly photographed the *Georges Leygues*, the *Gloire* and the *Montcalm*. The battleship *Richelieu*, a number of destroyers, submarines and smaller craft were also revealed. But the reconnaissance photographs showed something else: the *Richelieu* and the three cruisers at anchor with their awnings spread, and so positioned that they could not fire freely to seaward.[8] Spread awnings and a restricted field of fire certainly did not suggest that the French warships were expecting action. For Cunningham and Irwin, studying the reports on the flagship *Devonshire*, this posed an interesting question. Were the cruisers only temporarily at Dakar, and was Dakar, after all, not expecting the Allied attempt?

CHAPTER V

MENACE IN THE BALANCE

On Saturday 14th September the first of the Menace convoy steamed into Freetown harbour. Freetown, the capital of the then West African colony and protectorate of Sierra Leone, 500 miles south-east of Dakar, boasted the world's biggest harbour after Rio de Janeiro and Sydney—waters large enough to accommodate, at one period of the Second World War, 250 vessels including the *Queen Mary* and *Queen Elizabeth*. Now, as the *Westernland, Karanja* and other vessels slipped up the broad road-stead, Freetown harbour was crowded with Allied and neutral shipping of all kinds: warships, cargo boats, hospital ships, tankers, coasters, trawlers. Native boats laden with fruit and vegetables plied to and fro. The harbour's lush tropical surroundings made an attractive background. For the men of the *Ark Royal*, fresh from Gibraltar, it was a relief to see the green cloud-capped hills after the bareness of the Rock. But any hopes that, in this crossroads of news and rumour, the convoy's destination was still a secret were soon dispelled by the boys who paddled round the incoming ships in their dug-out canoes, ready to dive for coins thrown by the troops and shouting, 'Massa, you going Dakar?'[1]

'*Everybody* in Freetown knew of the projected expedition and raid on Dakar,' recalls Mr G. E. Higham, a member of the United Africa Company, who was then in Freetown awaiting a passage to England. 'And it was rumoured that the General

himself was in the town . . . It was only a long time later that
I heard that it was all supposed to have been a dark secret. But
it couldn't have been. There were scores of ships of all types in
Freetown harbour at the time making up convoys, etc. And—
stuck right in the middle of them all were two Japanese freight-
ers which were passing on the news to all and sundry, friend and
enemy alike, and there were plenty of the latter about, quite
apart from the Vichy French.'[2]

The real question now was: would the expedition ever get to
Dakar? The Vichy squadron's unexpected appearance on the
scene—whether or not its mission was to defend Dakar—had
threatened to upset the whole Menace plan. Instead of arriving
at Freetown as scheduled, to refuel and regroup in preparation
for the concerted move on Dakar, most of Cunningham's force
was away on a wild goose chase in the Atlantic, seeking to stop
the French ships from themselves entering Dakar. At the worst
the operation would have to be cancelled; at the best the
Menace time-table was being dangerously disrupted, with any
remaining security it may have had, fatally compromised.

Cunningham's force, after its fruitless quest, was not to reach
Freetown until early on the 17th. By then the future of Operation Menace was precarious indeed. But if external factors
were chiefly to blame, its own lack of organization did not exactly conduce to success. More blunders like those that had
marked the start of the expedition were now revealed. Partly because the British transports had originally been detailed for unopposed landings at the Cape Verde and Canary Islands, it was
now found that weapons and equipment essential for the Dakar
landing (which should have been 'tactically' loaded) were not
only scattered among different ships but so stowed that it was
virtually impossible to get them effectively re-sorted.

Then there was the case of the missing wireless set. On the
15th Captain Mitchell and others of the Spears Mission were
summoned to the *Westernland* to meet General Spears; and
Mitchell was told to call the Signals personnel from the *Karanja*
to bring over and install on the *Westernland* a powerful transmitting set—understood to be on the *Karanja*—that was to play

a vital part in communicating with London. Mitchell explained, to Spears' dismay, that the set was not on the *Karanja*. Spears then ordered an immediate search throughout the convoy. For three days Mitchell ferried from ship to ship with a search party, only to draw a blank. He tried the *Westernland* but was told that there were no papers or loading plan. From the *Karanja* he was referred to the *Ettrick*, but here too there were no papers and nobody knew exactly what was on board, and the set was said to be on the *Kenya*. The *Kenya's* quartermaster told him to try the *Karanja* again. In desperation he visited the *Sobieski*, without success. A signal to the *Pennland* brought a negative reply. Finally, on the 17th, Mitchell managed to borrow a No. 67 set from the *Ark Royal*.[3]

The original plan had been for a 48-hour stop at Freetown. The slow cargo-boat convoy, escorted by the *Savorgnan de Brazza*, had arrived as scheduled on the 15th. De Gaulle, intent on maintaining the highest state of readiness among his force, immediately inspected the *Savorgnan*, and next day toured the cargo boats. But now a growing cloud of uncertainty hung over the convoy. As the hours passed it idled on in Freetown harbour, without firm orders and beset by rumours and speculations about the Vichy ships. Anxious questions buzzed around the transports. Were the ships carrying Germans? Would an attempt against Dakar bring a French declaration of war? Would Operation Menace go ahead at all?

In London, on the 11th September, the news of the Vichy squadron's appearance had produced a shock of dismay. It was one more trouble for a War Cabinet that just then had its hands full with the gravest problem of all—the imminent invasion threat. For now, by every sign, invasion was a matter of hours away. Since the 7th September, when London's docks and East End had first been heavily attacked, the bombing of the capital had steadily intensified, and it was known that from the 8th to the 10th the conditions of moon and tide would be at their best for a seaborne landing. On the 8th the Cromwell alert (for a state of Readiness in Eastern and Southern Commands) had gone out, and on the 11th General Alan Brooke noted that 'evidence of impending invasion has been accumulating all day, more ships moving down the Channel.' And that day the Prime Minister broadcast to the nation a warning in the gravest terms. 'No one,' he said, 'should blind himself to the fact that a heavy full-scale invasion is being prepared with all the usual German thoroughness and method, and that it may be launched now . . . We must regard the next week or so as a very important period in our history.'[4]

Night and day the bombing went on, striking at the heart of London. On the 13th bombs fell on or around the Horse Guards, the House of Lords, the War Office; and Brooke noted: 'Everything looks like an invasion starting tomorrow from Thames to Plymouth.'[5] In this embattled atmosphere the War Cabinet and Chiefs of Staff now had to cope with the sudden Dakar complication. It was not the best moment to try to assess the right course of action in the light of swiftly moving events in a theatre 2,000 miles away. How great a threat to Operation Menace was the Vichy squadron? Should the operation be cancelled? Who should make the decision—the War Cabinet or the commanders on the spot? Throughout a hectic week of doubt and uncertainty the ether between London and Freetown buzzed with orders and counter-orders, queries and suggestions, representations and requests.

The first information of the Vichy squadron's movements— the *Hotspur*'s signal that she was shadowing the squadron east of Gibraltar—had reached the First Sea Lord, Admiral Sir Dudley Pound, in London on the morning of the 11th. Receiving it during a Chiefs of Staff meeting, he had promptly issued orders for the *Renown* and accompanying destroyers to raise steam, and reported to the War Cabinet. By this time the Vichy ships were well past the Straits. Thanks to the hold-up of the earlier Tangier and Madrid signals, vital hours had been lost. As so often, the difference between success and failure depended on a succession of 'ifs.' Churchill put it as follows: 'If the Consul-General (at Tangier) had marked the first message "Important", or if either of the admirals at Gibraltar, even though not in the secret, had so considered it themselves, or if the Foreign Office had been working normally, or if the Director of Operations had given the second message the priority which would have ensured the First Sea Lord's being woken up to read it immediately, the *Renown* could have stopped and parleyed with the French squadron pending decisive orders, which would certainly have been given by the War Cabinet, or, till they could be summoned, by me.'[6]

The French squadron's arrival at Dakar on the 14th was an added blow for the War Cabinet. The Chiefs of Staff had never been enthusiastic about Menace and now, at a hastily-called meeting on the 15th, they plainly wrote it off. They recommended instead that de Gaulle and his forces should sail on to Duala, in the French Cameroons, and from there proceed to Chad (already declared for de Gaulle), where they would be welcomed. Meanwhile the British troops would return to England.[7] This was agreed next day at a War Cabinet meeting at which Churchill outlined the unhappy chain of events which amounted, as he put it, to a 'fiasco'.[8] For the Premier, always and above all a fighter, to have to accept Menace as a failure, was a bitter pill. At this grave moment for the Allies he had staked much on it. Even after the escape of the French ships from Casablanca he was reluctant to jettison the operation. But when the effort to stop them entering Dakar failed, he had to regard the fate of Menace as sealed. 'I had no doubt whatever that it should be abandoned,' he wrote.[9]

So, on the 16th September, by consent of the political and military chiefs in London, Operation Menace was cancelled. From Sir Alexander Cadogan, Permanent Under-Secretary of State at the Foreign Office, came a perhaps representative Foreign Office view. 'The French ships have forestalled us in Dakar, and so "Menace" is off!' he noted on the 16th. 'I cannot truly say I am sorry!'[10]

At 2 pm that day a signal went off from London to the Dakar force at Freetown.[11] 'His Majesty's Government,' it began, 'have decided that presence of French cruisers at Dakar renders the execution of Dakar operation impracticable.' It went on to dismiss the feasibility of a landing at Konakri (de Gaulle's originally proposed landing-point) and to state that a close blockade of Dakar from the seaward was impossible with the naval forces available. It then advocated, as the best plan, that de Gaulle's force should land at Duala. 'Unless General de Gaulle has any strong objections to the latter course,' the signal ended, 'it should be put into operation forthwith.'

But, as it quickly appeared, de Gaulle—and with him Spears and the British commanders—had the strongest objections. Within hours they had all fired off cables to London registering disagreement. Spears' first angry reaction, jotted in his diary that day expressed his own personal feeling. 'Here are people,' he wrote, 'who didn't fear to run the risk of a naval battle with only part of our naval forces under the most unfavourable circumstances imaginable, that is, only British ships against the French, who now have cold feet when these same ships are helpless under awnings! Terrible blow to de Gaulle!'[12]

De Gaulle was in fact deeply shocked. He saw the cancellation of Menace as 'the worst possible solution.' He felt that if the attempt on Dakar were abandoned, Vichy would merely have to wait for the British fleet to return northwards before resuming its efforts to spread its influence in Equatorial Africa. With no naval opposition, the French cruisers would hurry south, and if the Free French moved down to Duala as proposed by the War Cabinet, they would be caught up in a futile struggle in the African bush against fellow-Frenchmen. He was therefore convinced that Operation Menace should go forward.

Early on the 17th he sent off a strongly-worded cable to Churchill: 'Having been informed of the new and negative decision with regard to Operation Menace, I wish to insist to you personally and formally that the plan for the reconstitution of French Africa through Dakar should be upheld and carried out. This is particularly essential on account of the reactions from Vichy which threaten to undermine the present favourable attitude of the great majority in Africa. It is also of vital importance from the point of view of the morale of the French population of Africa who will inevitably get to know of the arrival at Freetown both of myself and of the British forces. It is of even greater importance from the point of view of the general conduct of the war which demands, in my opinion, that the Allies should gain control, before the enemy do so, of the air, naval and military bases of French Africa particularly in North Africa. At the very least, should the British Government now uphold its new and negative decision concerning the direct action upon Dakar by sea, I request the immediate co-operation of the British naval and air forces here present to support and cover an operation which I personally shall conduct with my own troops against Dakar from the interior, proceeding from Kaolack via Thiès.'[13]

At sea on the flagship *Devonshire*, heading for Freetown, Cunningham and Irwin were likewise firmly against cancellation. In their view, unless the arrival of the Vichy ships at Dakar was found to have markedly raised local morale, their presence there left the existing naval position virtually unchanged. Two of the cruisers were badly berthed for firing seawards, all three were under awnings and all presented first class bombing targets. In this sense they had cabled Churchill on the evening of the 16th.

Simultaneously with de Gaulle, Spears was mounting his own broadside to the Prime Minister: 'One, if changes in policy are often puzzling in London they are heartbreaking here. Two, it is impossible to understand why naval action under most unfavourable circumstances, British alone against French, was boldly faced on Friday whereas on Monday the prospect of tackling these same French ships now lying helplessly in harbour under awnings is considered impracticable. Three, De Gaulle's presence here must inevitably be known, and it is quite clear that if he fails to seize opportunity so obviously within his grasp of rallying West Africa, and agrees to vegetate at Duala, his power to rally any other part of the French Empire is gone for ever. Four, if fleet departs leaving de Gaulle here, the accusation of having abandoned him to his fate will swing French opinion totally against us in France as well as in Africa. Five, authoritative opinion here is that unless Dakar muzzled, all gains must eventually be lost, whilst Vichy forces becoming ever more hostile under enemy influence will threaten our repeat our colonies. Freetown, where over 60 ships now lying is under an hour's flight from important French aerodrome at Konakri. Six, . . Am immensely relieved to know Commanders M Force signalled London, even before opportunity consultation, in sense of these opinions which are held by all here.'[14]

The British commanders' signal was the first to reach Churchill, and it gave him a pleasant surprise. 'It was very rare at this stage of the war,' he wrote, 'for commanders on the spot to press for audacious courses. Usually the pressure to run risks came from home . . . If the men on the spot thought it was a time to do and dare, we should certainly give them a free hand.' He therefore gladly took them at their word, and just before midnight on the 16th cabled them as follows: 'You are fully at liberty to consider the whole situation yourselves and consult de Gaulle, and we shall carefully consider then any advice you may give.'[15]

So, with the Prime Minister swayed by the powerful representations of the men on the spot, the cancellation of Operation Menace was rescinded. Tuesday 17th September saw crucial meetings of the War Cabinet and the expedition's leaders at Freetown to consider the matter further and reach a firm and final decision.

At the War Cabinet that morning Churchill reported the latest developments and affirmed that, though he himself thought the operation should be cancelled, it was as well to hear the views of the commanders.[16] There was a further meeting at 9 pm—in the middle of an air-raid—by which time de Gaulle's and Spears' hard-hitting cables had been received. Coming as they did on top of the British commanders' signal, Ministers were strongly impressed by their arguments. Churchill was now moving in favour of pursuing Menace, on the grounds that the War Cabinet did not seriously expect any hostile reactions from Vichy. Eden, Sinclair and Greenwood supported him. Neville Chamberlain, making his last recorded speech at a War Cabinet meeting, believed that if Menace were abandoned nothing could prevent the collapse of the Free French movement in West Africa. Attlee, too, was prepared to see Menace go forward.[17] Sir Alexander Cadogan, who was present, was not so certain about it. He recorded: 'Messages show people on spot want to go on with Menace. I warned against possible result of another Oran. But everyone in favour.'[18]

As a result, the War Cabinet agreed that 'if the Commanders on the spot, Admiral Cunningham, General Irwin, General de Gaulle—who were in the best position to judge the situation—were, after full consideration, in favour of proceeding with Operation Menace, in its original form (or in its original form subject to minor modifications), they were authorized by the War Cabinet to go ahead.'[19] Responsibility was now firmly on the shoulders of the men at Freetown.

Meanwhile, early on the 17th at Freetown, the British commanders, who had just arrived from their vain quest for the Vichy squadron, were in close conference with de Gaulle and Spears on the *Westernland*. De Gaulle insisted on the need for early action at Dakar. He still believed that he could expect substantial support in the town provided agents could be sent in to boost it, action was prompt and the British part in the operation not over-emphasized. His agents, he said, were ready at Bathurst and fully briefed. He now proposed that the original plan to enter Dakar harbour peaceably should go ahead, and that if this failed, Free French troops should attempt to land at nearby Rufisque, with naval and air support if necessary, and from there advance on Dakar. British troops would be landed in support only if called upon after a bridgehead had been established.

This Rufisque scheme, to be known as Plan Charles, was further discussed by de Gaulle and Irwin. De Gaulle believed it would be a useful intermediate action betwen the sending of his envoys and the landing of a British force. Moreover, it solved the problem of how to employ the main body of his own troops. At first Irwin saw objections to it. 'When I pointed out that this might lead to a major clash between Frenchmen,' he recorded, 'de Gaulle accepted the risk and committed himself to complete co-operation with British troops in case of need, and did not shirk the responsibility of fighting between Frenchmen.'[20] This was a major change of attitude by de Gaulle. He was now accepting the grim possibility that hitherto he had been so anxious to avoid. The scheme was put to Cunningham, who agreed and issued the necessary naval orders. Plan Charles, belatedly and hastily conceived, would play a major but ill-fated part in the first day's Menace operations.

Cunningham cabled a report of the meeting to London late on the 17th, and added: 'After careful consideration of all factors, we are of the opinion that the presence of these three cruisers has not sufficiently increased the risks, which were always accepted, to justify abandonment of the enterprise. We accordingly recommend acceptance of de Gaulle's new proposal, and that, should he fail, landing of British troops should be undertaken to install him as previously contemplated. Increased strength in (our) naval forces is however considered essential. The operation should be carried out four days after decision of His Majesty's Government is received.'[21]

Hitherto the most doubtful member of the Anglo-French command on the prospects of Menace had been General Irwin. Now even Irwin was converted. He signalled the CIGS at the War Office: 'As you know, I have already accepted risks in this operation not fully justified on purely military grounds. New information possibly increases those risks, but I consider them worth accepting in view of obvious results of success. De Gaulle has also committed himself to complete co-operation with British troops in case of need, and he has not shirked responsibility for fighting between Frenchmen.'[22]

Cunningham's cable reached the Admiralty at 7.55 am on the 18th. The War Cabinet, meeting at noon, considered it and confirmed the Cabinet go-ahead decision of the night before. At 1.20 pm the following signal went off from the Admiralty: 'We give you full authority to go ahead and do what you think is best in order to give effect to the original purpose of the expedition. Keep us informed.'[23]

So now, after seven days of doubt and hesitation on the part of the War Cabinet the decision was made.* The commanders' view had prevailed; and despite the unforeseen risks presented by the arrival of the Vichy squadron at Dakar, the disruption to the operation's time-table caused thereby, and the possible loss of all surprise, Operation Menace was finally to proceed.

Now, with the Vichy cruisers adding their potential fire-power to the defences, Menace was more than ever a gamble. It says much for the resolve of the three Anglo-French commanders that, faced with the new threat, they did not call the expedition off. The War Cabinet had left the door open for them to do so without discredit. But against the increased risks now facing them, the commanders were still relying on one hope. Discounting the Cassandra-like warnings of Poulter and Rushbrooke, they were still calculating that pro-Free French support in Dakar, a fifth column mobilized by Gaullist agents from outside, would be enough to overcome any opposition to de Gaulle's entry.

On the *Westernland*, de Gaulle himself was still hopeful of a largely unopposed landing at Dakar. Despite everything, he remained confident of effective support within the town. He had so expressed himself at the commanders' meeting on the 17th. And to support his views, an Intelligence report arrived from the British Consul, St Vincent, Cape Verde Islands, that same day.[24] 'Feeling for de Gaulle very strong and (supporters) would fight for him if strong lead shown,' this stated. 'Feeling for British one of distrust and indecision. No faith whatsoever in Vichy Government, French newspapers or radio.'

The rest of the report was of more direct operational interest. It said: '*Richelieu* in dock, extensive repairs to hull effected and

* The record of 'stop and go' ran like this: 11th September, Cabinet learns of Gibraltar break-out and Admiralty belatedly orders Somerville to contact Vichy ships in Atlantic; 15th, Chiefs of Staff recommend abandonment of Menace on learning of Vichy ships' arrival at Dakar on 14th, and advocate alternative plan; 16th, Cabinet confirms this and notifies Menace commanders at Freetown. Commanders reply strongly opposing decision; 17th, Cabinet re-considers and authorizes Commanders to go ahead if they think fit. Meanwhile Cunningham cables London that abandonment is not justified; 18th, Cabinet, on receipt of this, gives Commanders full authority to proceed with Menace.

in hand. Engine room severely damaged, French estimate possible speed 17 knots. Warships: 7 destroyers, 1 light cruiser, 1 gunboat, no subs seen. Another source says 2 large modern French subs in harbour with orders to scuttle if Germans attempt to seize; if British attack they will resist.' As to Defence: 'All British vessels to be fired on if within 20 miles of port, range of batteries approx. 14 miles. Airplanes stated 10 Martin bombers and 40–50 Curtiss fighters. Another source states 200 to 300 all of which arrived since the collapse.' Finally: 'Merchant vessels at least 25 in port. 3 or 4 German officers who act for armistice committee receiving their orders from Wiesbaden. All fuel supplies are controlled. Flour, sugar, staple foods scarce.'

The starkly anti-British attitude here revealed was not encouraging for the British commanders. But the report seemed to confirm de Gaulle's optimistic views. As for the 'strong lead' needed to mobilize supporters, that was already on the way. Soon after de Gaulle's arrival at Freetown, his envoy Boislambert had reported to him, fresh from his successful rallying of the Cameroons. On the 16th he had sent Boislambert off to Dakar, confident he could repeat the process there. With Boislambert went two companions, Lt Brunel and Midshipman Akoub. Travelling by air to Bathurst, in Gambia, they were to continue by native canoe to French territory and thence make their way to Dakar. Their main mission was to contact certain highly-placed sympathizers and sabotage military communications. These preliminary moves, together with the appearance off-shore of the Anglo-French armada and the leaflet and radio appeals that were planned to precede the actual landing would, de Gaulle fondly hoped, suffice to ensure a friendly welcome from the people of Dakar. But Operation Menace was now due to be launched in a matter of days, and much depended on whether Boislambert could report back the results of his efforts before the expedition left Freetown. If he could not, the uncertainty about the strength of Vichy opposition still remained.

CHAPTER VI

'LET THINGS RIP'

In the steamy heat of Freetown harbour the waiting and uncertainty were bearing hard on French and British alike. The
commanders themselves were becoming strained and edgy.
During the long conferences in airless cabins there were clear
signs of frayed patience, as differences arose between the
British chiefs and de Gaulle, backed by Spears. Unguarded
remarks led to hot words, followed by apologies. There was a
sharp clash over the role Spears might play in the landing, and
a major row flared over the thorny question of command responsibility. Spears tells the story in his diary for the 18th September.[1]

'All morning and hot part of afternoon taken up with discussions with Irwin. I thought de Gaulle was accommodating,
as he was yesterday . . . We were still working at tea time
when Cunningham sent for us. There was to start with a
passage I greatly resented. It arose I imagine out of previous
discussions between Cunningham and Irwin as to whether I
should land or not.*

* This referred to the possibility of Spears himself landing at Dakar, as de
Gaulle's envoy, if d'Argenlieu's mission failed—d'Argenlieu being de Gaulle's
original choice for approaching the Dakar leaders with his personal letter
requesting the entry of the Free French. It was thought that while the French
might fire on fellow-Frenchmen, they would not do so on a British general
in uniform. The objection to the plan was that this would give the operation
a British appearance and minimize de Gaulle's role, which was admitted to

'Cunningham talked of "Commissars" and what was my role—(my signal about the operation being put off, whilst vastly impressing and placating the commanders made them feel on second thoughts they might, in the future, be the victims). In this connection a signal came in during the evening from Alexander [First Lord of the Admiralty] saying it was not fear of extra force that had led to cancellation of the operation, but apprehension lest the morale at Dakar would be heightened by arrival of cruisers; as if they could judge in London!

'I didn't take this personal matter up till our discussion was over, but then did so with both Irwin and Cunningham. We were asked to dine on *Devonshire* and I said I wouldn't come, greatly resenting what was said. Profuse apologies: Cunningham said he only tried to be funny. Left it at that. A sumptuous dinner for these parts in *Devonshire*. Quite pleasant evening, then bomb dropped. Irwin asked de Gaulle to sign copy of Instructions. All the amendments had been signed save one, the most important, and I didn't draw any attention. De Gaulle has a keen eye and spotted it at once.

'They had left in the words "Command of this expedition is exercised jointly by Vice-Admiral Cunningham and Major-General Irwin . . ." No mention of de Gaulle. He flatly refused to sign. I backed him. There was considerable asperity. De Gaulle's point was that it was inadmissible that it should be said he had no say in the command of an expedition in which he played so prominent a part. That in fact in every hypothesis envisaged he, de Gaulle, played a most prominent part with his troops, and to deny this was to deny a plain fact. There was a further point which I made: these Instructions will become a historical document: from them it would appear for ever that this was purely a British expedition in which de Gaulle was a mere puppet.

'Irwin pressed me and so did Cunningham, but neither de Gaulle nor I would budge—when Cunningham said to me

---

be highly undesirable. It was therefore decided that Spears would land only if d'Argenlieu or the Dakar authorities asked for him, but not if d'Argenlieu's mission failed.

meaningfully, "We sail the day after tomorrow—are you coming?" I said we had better put off the discussion until tomorrow. There had been some talk previously about the British carrying on alone. So we left, de Gaulle naturally deeply resentful, and—this is the fate of the liaison officer always—not so keen on me though I had fought his case harder than he had.

'One thing is quite clear—the commanders, although they welcome my backing d'Argenlieu if he or the French at Dakar ask for me, won't have me going ashore as representing purely British interests should d'Argenlieu fail: this although Cunningham himself says I am the only person who could do so. I went so far as to say he was opposed to this unless I got specific orders from home. I said I would ask for no such orders and wouldn't think of going ashore unless they agreed; the proposal was based on the idea of avoiding the shedding of blood. That theirs was the responsibility for cutting out this measure.'

Next day Spears received 'an extraordinarily nice letter from Cunningham, which more than made amends for what occurred last night.' Later the admiral visited Spears and 'said some very nice things and wanted to make certain there wasn't the shadow or the substance of a misunderstanding.' 'Irwin, who didn't shine in all this,' added Spears, 'made no sign all day . . .'[2] Cunningham was a much harassed man and in the existing tensions the tiff about Spears' role in the operation was understandable. More serious was the dispute over de Gaulle's part in the command of the expedition. Sensitive as the general was about any attempt to play down his importance as a leader of the expedition, nothing was more likely to offend him than the omission of his name as one of its joint commanders. It was typical of his insistence on maintaining his status as an independent leader that he had refused the invitation to join the British commanders on the *Devonshire* en route to Freetown. But the tough line taken by him and Spears now received its reward. An amended Order was swiftly produced giving him all he wanted. He was named, alongside Cunningham and Irwin, as a joint commander of Operation Menace.

Under the heading 'Command' the amended Instructions now ran: 'The employment of a part or whole of the Free French Forces in co-operation with British Naval and Military Forces shall be subject to mutual agreement between General de Gaulle, Commander Free French Forces, Vice-Admiral J. H. D. Cunningham, C.B., M.V.O., Commander Naval Forces, and Major-General N. M. S. Irwin, C.B., D.S.O., M.C., Commander Military Forces.

'When Free French Troops are co-operating with British Naval and Military Forces the Command of the whole Combined Forces will be exercised jointly by Vice-Admiral Cunningham, Major-General N. M. S. Irwin and General de Gaulle subject to the over-riding condition that except when placed specifically under Command of one or other of the joint Commanders, the British Commanders jointly or severally will not exercise Command over Free French Troops without the consent of General de Gaulle, nor will General de Gaulle exercise Command over any British Naval or Military Forces.'[3]

It was further stated that where orders in writing were issued to the Free French Naval Forces, they would, whenever possible, receive General de Gaulle's covering approval. And it was specified that the decision as to whether Free French Troops, when operating on land with British Troops, should be placed under the local British Commander's Command, would be given jointly by Irwin and de Gaulle. All this was calculated to meet de Gaulle's most exacting requirements. And he had the final satisfaction of being placed as the first of the three signatories to the document.

The plans for Operation Menace had now been finally hammered out. In essence they were the same as those detailed by Churchill in early August. The Anglo-French armada would approach Dakar during darkness, with de Gaulle's ships leading. At dawn leaflets would be dropped on the town, while Free French airmen from the *Ark Royal* would land at Ouakam, the local airfield, to parley with the French officers on the spot. If well received, they would then drive to Dakar harbour to

meet de Gaulle's envoys from the *Westernland*, led by d'Argenlieu, who meanwhile would be entering harbour in a launch
bearing the French tricolour and a white flag. D'Argenlieu's
party would proceed in the car used by the airmen to the
residence of Dakar's Governor-General, Pierre Boisson, to
present the letter from de Gaulle.

Meanwhile, on the *Westernland*, de Gaulle would be broad-
casting to the people of Dakar, and the British fleet would be
closing on Dakar to present a show of force. These moves, aided
by the preliminary efforts of Boislambert's group, would, it was
hoped, be enough to persuade the authorities to receive de
Gaulle and declare for the Free French cause. In the event of
opposition, Plan Charles (the Free French landing at Rufisque)
would be put into action. And to cover the various possible
situations that might arise, a set of code-words had been evolved
by Cunningham's CSO, Captain Walter. 'Happy' would signify
a friendly reception and that all had gone well. 'Sticky' would
mean that de Gaulle's peaceful entry was meeting partial
resistance and some support was required. 'Nasty' would in-
dicate an unquestionably hostile reception, calling for a full-
scale assault (bombardment and a British landing). The British
landing plans in the case of 'Nasty' were three: 'Conqueror',
landings at Rufisque and Hann; 'William', a main landing at
Hann; and 'Rufus', a landing at Rufisque.

All now seemed set for the operation. Launching-date was
fixed for Monday the 23rd, and the fleet would leave Freetown
for Dakar on the 21st. Throughout the waiting warships and
transports there was general relief that the waiting and sus-
pense were over. The Free French particularly welcomed the
prospect of action at last. But not all of them impressed their
British colleagues. Those aboard the *Ark Royal* with their two
Luciole aircraft, in preparation for their flying mission, seemed
restless and unresponsive. 'In spite of the best efforts of their
hosts,' one officer noted, 'the new arrivals showed little signs of
settling down, wandering disconsolately about the ship,
grumbling at the arrangements made on their behalf . . . The
tiny Luciole aircraft were dirty and badly maintained, but

soon looked better under the attention of the Fleet Air Arm. The Free French officers (were) a mixed lot, but it was clear that they were determined to continue in the war, even if this meant fighting their compatriots.'[4]

But even now the fates were dogging Menace. With 48 hours to go before sailing came a new shock for the commanders. On the 19th news reached Freetown that the Vichy squadron had left Dakar. The cruiser *Australia*, on patrol, had spotted it some 250 miles west of Freetown, heading south-east. The report was flashed to London, and the Admiralty's reaction was swift and unequivocal: carry out Menace as soon as possible, if necessary pursuing the French ships northwards, but not so far as to compromise the operation. For Cunningham this meant another chase, another infuriating disruption of plans. On receiving the order he hurried to the *Westernland* to inform de Gaulle and Spears that he was leaving at once to intercept the cruisers and sink them if they resisted. At de Gaulle's request he agreed to take d'Argenlieu with him again on the *Devonshire*, carrying a message from the Free French leader to Admiral Bourrague. Spears noted Cunningham's mood: 'terrific determination now.'[5]

At least the Vichy cruisers' move meant a weakening of Dakar's defences. But the news only brought de Gaulle new worries. 'I could have no doubt,' he wrote later, 'that this powerful naval force was bound for Equatorial Africa, where the port of Libreville was open to it, and where they would find it easy to re-take Pointe Noire and Duala. If such a thunderclap did not suffice to reverse the situation in the Congo and Cameroons, these magnificent ships could easily cover the transport and landing of forces of repression from Dakar, Konakri or Abidjan (Ivory Coast).'[6] He had of course deduced correctly: he might win Dakar more easily, but only at the heavy price of losing his earlier gains farther south. He therefore vigorously backed Cunningham in his resolve to stop the French Squadron at once.

One thing was now increasingly obvious: the cruisers' arrival at Dakar had had nothing to do with Operation

Menace. But this had not become apparent to the members of
the War Cabinet in London. At a meeting on the 19th to consider the matter it was assumed that the cruisers had, in Churchill's words, 'carried Vichy-minded troops, technicians and
authorities to Dakar.' 'The possibilities of a vigorous resistance
were increased out of all proportion to the new forces involved,' he added. 'There would certainly be sharp fighting.
All my colleagues shared my instincts to let things rip.'[7]

But for the Menace commanders letting things rip was
becoming an ever more complicated business. As Cunningham's
force raced out into the Atlantic to head off the Vichy squadron,
it was being side-tracked from its real assignment for the second
time. And Operation Menace was showing unhappy signs of
getting out of hand.

Churchill was wrong in his conviction that the Vichy ships
were bringing reinforcements to Dakar. Their purpose in calling there, apart from the need to refuel, was in fact to embark a Senegalese detachment to strengthen the defences in
Equatorial Africa and the Gabon. And since their arrival on
the 14th the local authorities had been anxious for the cruisers
to press on south with all speed. The urgency of the move was
dictated by the reports of successful Free French rallyings in
the Gabon by de Gaulle's agent, de Larminat, and of increased
British naval activity in the area. Serious note was taken of the
arrival at Pointe Noire (Equatorial Africa), on 6th September,
of the cruiser *Delhi*.[8] While an Anglo-French clash was to be
avoided at all costs, it was felt imperative to show the French
flag with the minimum of delay. Pierre Boisson, the Governor-
General at Dakar, therefore decided that Bourrague should
hurry to Libreville and then visit Pointe Noire, and possibly
Duala in the Gabon.

Admiral Bourrague prepared to sail from Dakar on the
evening of the 18th. Steaming at 17 knots, his squadron would
reach Libreville on the 26th. And, if confirmation were wanted
that Vichy was still unaware of Operation Menace, at noon
on the 18th Bourrague received a signal from Admiral Platon,

Vichy's Minister for the Colonies, ordering him to act energetically to re-establish Vichy control at Pointe Noire and Duala simultaneously. He therefore hastened his preparations and left port at 6 pm.

An extraordinary situation was now developing. Bourrague's squadron was moving south from Dakar to restore and maintain the Vichy cause in French Equatorial Africa, while Cunningham's force was about to move north to Dakar to plant the Free French flag in French West Africa. They would, within a day or so of each other, actually traverse the same sea lanes in opposite directions. The advantage in this strange tale of cross-purposes was, in theory at least, with Cunningham. He knew the Vichy squadron was on the move south and could deduce what its purpose must be, whereas Admiral Bourrague and the Dakar authorities still seemed ignorant of the Anglo-French plan to assault Dakar. Or was it that they knew, and were fully prepared for it? But for Cunningham time was running out. To stop and turn back Bourrague's ships he would have to waste precious hours—hours in which Operation Menace might well lose its vital element of surprise and find itself encountering a defence at last forewarned.

But the Vichy squadron was not Cunningham's only target. Before it left Dakar on the 18th, three other vessels had put out in support of its mission. Late on the 14th the petrol tanker *Tarn*, escorted by the cruiser *Primauguet*, had sailed for Gabon with fuel to replenish the Vichy cruisers' tanks on their arrival there. And on the 15th the cargo-boat *Poitiers* left with a 1,700-ton mixed cargo for Libreville and other ports. None of these ships was to reach their destination. They were to run into the warships which Cunningham had left watching the area when he returned to Freetown.

On the 16th the *Poitiers* was stopped 100 miles from Dakar by the *Cumberland*. Fearing capture, the commander gave orders to scuttle and embarked his crew into life-boats. The *Cumberland* replied by firing two shots across the boats' bows to stop them, took the crew prisoner and completed the sinking of the *Poitiers* by gunfire. For the commanders at Freetown—on the point of

deciding to recommend going ahead with Operation Menace—
this was sobering news. 'They are a bit shaken in their resolve,'
Spears noted on the 17th, 'by the fact that a French cargo set
herself on fire rather than surrender to a British warship off
Dakar.'[9]

CHAPTER VII

ANOTHER DIVERSION

Two days later the tanker *Tarn* and her escorting cruiser *Primauguet*, now well to the south-east of Dakar and some 640 miles from Libreville, were to encounter trouble. About noon on the 19th the *Primauguet* spotted two British warships away to starboard. Her commander, Captain Goybet, had suspected he was being trailed for some days. Now, certain of this, he called his crew to action stations and gave the order to keep steaming. But the warships—the cruisers *Cornwall* and *Delhi*—closed in and directed him to stop.

The *Delhi* signalled him that she was sending a launch across, with an important message. Shortly after, two naval officers and a signaller boarded the *Primauguet*, and one of them handed Captain Goybet three letters, one from de Gaulle and the two others from the *Cornwall's* commander, Captain Hamill. De Gaulle's letter, transmitted in cipher to the *Cornwall* from Freetown with orders to deliver it to Captain Goybet, was a copy of that written by him on 13th September and entrusted to d'Argenlieu to present to Admiral Bourrague. It was the ultimatum directing the admiral to place himself under de Gaulle's orders and return to Casablanca or take the consequences. Now Goybet read it, and replied tersely that de Gaulle had no official status with the French Government and therefore no right to intervene against his instructions. At the same time Captain Hamill had been directed to give Goybet his own 'ultimatum'.

4. Admiral Sir John Cunningham, Joint Commander of the Dakar Expedition

5. Two Vichy anti-Churchill cartoon posters referring to Dakar and Mers-el-Kebir

This stated that on the orders of the British Admiralty no French naval forces could be authorized to sail to a French West African port. It went on: 'I have received the order to use force if necessary to ensure the execution of these instructions, and I shall not hesitate to do this, but I hope that you will agree with me that we shall both serve our countries by avoiding the development of such a crisis. That is why I ask you to turn your ship about immediately and return to Casablanca.'[1]

But Captain Hamill knew and admired the French Navy and the thought of having to fire on French ships was highly repugnant to him. So, along with his official letter, he had sent Goybet a personal message in much warmer terms. It ran:

'Captain: It is a painful thing for me to find myself in a situation in which I am forced to give you this ultimatum. During three years as Naval Attaché in Paris I have grown to regard myself as a brother of the French Navy, and it is incredible to me that we are no longer united in our firm purpose of fighting the Germans with all our resources. Perhaps you will come and join us. I hope so, but it is a very difficult decision for you, and this letter is written not as a piece of propaganda but out of friendship. I hope with all my heart that you will find it possible to do what I ask, and put in to Casablanca without forcing me to do what I shall regret for the rest of my life. If you can help me by avoiding an "incident" you will indeed deserve the gratitude of your country and also that of the true friends of the French Navy, among whom it is my great desire to continue to be numbered . . . M. Hamill.'[2]

Hamill's appeal underlined a conflict between duty and friendship inherent in the grim situation of those months, which had turned old allies into virtual enemies. But if Goybet was tempted to read any weakness into his letter he was quickly disabused by the officer who had brought it, and who now made plain that his commander would not hesitate to open fire if necessary. Goybet briefly considered the odds. He was confident his men would resist if he gave the order, but he knew that the *Cornwall* would make short work of the *Primauguet* and *Tarn* if it came to a fight. And no possible advantage could be gained by the loss of the ships. Even so, before obeying Captain Hamill's orders he decided to obtain authorization from Admiral Bourrague. Hamill reluctantly allowed this and gave him until 5 pm to receive Bourrague's reply.

So at 3 pm Admiral Bourrague, on his flagship *Georges Leygues* heading the southbound cruiser squadron, now 21 hours out of Dakar, received this signal: 'An ultimatum from *Cornwall* and a cruiser type *Delhi* forces us to fight or make course for Casablanca from 5 pm. In view of international importance of decision to be taken, ask for your precise instructions.'[3] Immediately Bourrague realized his helplessness. He was 1,000 miles away from the *Primauguet* and *Tarn* and could not possibly reach them in time to be of help. There was nothing for it but to instruct Goybet to obey the *Cornwall*'s commander and turn about for Casablanca. So just after 4 pm he signalled Goybet accordingly.

But, as Bourrague well knew, this was not just a setback for the *Primauguet* and *Tarn*. It spelt failure for him, his squadron and his whole enterprise. For without the *Tarn*'s fuel to refill his rapidly emptying tanks at Libreville, he would be powerless to carry on. Even if he decided after all to make for Libreville, it was clear that he would be forcibly prevented by the British warships, which were now showing themselves determined to stop French vessels entering French Equatorial ports. Weighing the situation, he saw that for him too there was no alternative but to turn back. So at 5.50 pm he signalled his superiors at Dakar, informing them of his decision.

Bourrague's squadron had already been sighted by the British some hours before. The cruiser *Cumberland* had spotted it at 9 am off Cape Bissua and set a parallel course 25,000 yards to starboard. She was quickly joined by the *Australia*. The two cruisers then dogged the squadron until nightfall. Bourrague had likewise sighted them, and no doubt their presence confirmed his resolve to turn about and avoid the danger of a clash. But to throw the British off the scent he had decided to continue southwards until dark and then swing around under cover of night. About 6.30 he ordered a 180-degree turn and increased speed to 29 knots. But he failed to elude the British cruisers. They turned too and followed the fleeing squadron back towards Dakar, *Cumberland* leading. As the strange pursuit went on, Bourrague ordered his crews to be ready to open fire on the *Cumberland*. But he had little or no intention of going to such a dire extremity. He was really trying to play for time. He signalled the *Cumberland*: 'What would you do if I went to Pointe-Noire?' The *Cumberland* replied that Cunningham would have to be consulted. Meanwhile the Vichy ships were maintaining full speed, in the hope that if this parleying with the *Cumberland* could be kept up they would have time to reach the cover of the Dakar forts, still some 12 hours' steaming away.

Then, as they were somewhere off the African coast at Konakri, trouble struck them. The *Gloire*'s engines failed. Not long before, her commander, Captain Broussignac, had signalled the flagship *Georges Leygues* that all was going well and she could if necessary increase her speed. Minutes later, from the *Gloire*'s engine-room came the report of a fault—cause unknown. Speed steadily dropped from 20 knots until the *Gloire* was hardly moving. Steaming not far behind her in company with the *Cumberland*, the *Australia* had noted this odd behaviour, and now turned a powerful searchlight on her and sent out a puzzled request to know what she was doing. And as the harassed Broussignac, caught in this awkward predicament, was considering scuttling rather than fall into British hands, two British destroyers had raced forward to flank the *Gloire* on each side.

Meanwhile, on the *Georges Leygues*, Bourrague faced an acute dilemma. Should he stop in order to stand by the *Gloire*, or should the *Georges Leygues* and *Montcalm* head on for Dakar without her? He decided to write off the *Gloire* and carry on: in this way two at least of his squadron would have a good chance of evading the British and gaining Dakar. So, leaving the *Gloire* to her fate, the *Georges Leygues* and *Montcalm* sped on northwards. Astern of them still hurried the *Cumberland*. In this queer Anglo-French encounter (it could hardly be called an action), so fraught with political complications, the last thing either side wanted was to resort to shooting—certainly not to start it. Thus the *Cumberland*'s commander, in his efforts to stop Bourrague's cruisers, found himself having to act more like a diplomat than a fighting sailor. All he could do was to keep following, and continue sending the admiral persuasive messages, couched in carefully friendly terms.

At 11.55 pm he signalled: 'My Government instructs me to inform you that it cannot allow you to re-enter Dakar because it considers it under German control. You must either come back with me to Freetown to discuss matter or make your way to Casablanca under escort. Surely we can find a better way than that of fighting each other.'

Minutes later Bourrague's answer came: 'I give you the assurance that in no case will my cruisers pass under German authority.' The *Cumberland* flashed back: 'I will immediately inform my admiral of your message.' Thirty-five minutes later the *Cumberland* sent another appeal: 'I am very anxious that the representative of my commander-in-chief should have the chance to discuss with you before there is any chance of an incident which we will both regret. Would you agree to a meeting at sea at which my admiral could send a representative by plane to meet you? I pray you to consider this as being very much to our mutual advantage. I believe your colleague the *Gloire* is in process of discussion at this moment farther south.' Back came Bourrague's reply: 'I am most grateful for your proposal which I am transmitting immediately to my chiefs. I think in fact this solution could be advantageous.'[4]

But as the messages flashed to and fro in the dark Atlantic night, it was clear that Bourrague was stalling. Through the small hours his ships sped on northwards, intent only on reaching Dakar. For the *Cumberland* it was becoming increasingly obvious that the chase was fruitless. This was realised, too, at Freetown. And at 0246 a signal reached the British cruiser instructing her to return to Freetown if she was unable to prevent the Vichy ships entering Dakar. Leaving her quarry, the *Cumberland* turned about and made for Freetown. And at 7.30 am on the 20th the *Georges Leygues* and *Montcalm*, clear of all pursuit, passed Dakar's protective boom and entered port—just over 36 hours after they had left.

Meanwhile, some 200 miles to the south, the fate of the disabled *Gloire* had been decided. Captain Broussignac would not have to give the dire order to scuttle: the British had directed that his ship was to proceed to Casablanca, and there was nothing for him but to agree. So, at 2.30 am on the 20th, limping at 4 knots, the *Gloire* headed north on the long voyage. To give her a send-off, steaming alongside was the destroyer *Inglefield*, one of Cunningham's force. Aboard her was de Gaulle's envoy, d'Argenlieu, who had transferred from the *Devonshire* at Cunningham's request to communicate a message from de Gaulle. Now, bawling from a loud-speaker, d'Argenlieu transmitted it across the water: 'Am informed of your attitude and your situation. I wish to tell you that if you want to return to Freetown to refuel or for any other reason, you may do so. In this case I give you my word of honour that you and your crew may remain freely aboard your ship and that you will then be able, if you wish, to return to Casablanca.'[5]

Thus informed—though it is doubtful if Broussignac or his dejected crew were in the mood to pay much attention—the *Gloire* moved away through the darkness, escorted by the *Australia*. Next morning she picked up to 11 knots, and by afternoon was managing 17. Soon after, nearing the sea area of Dakar, the *Australia* was to question the *Gloire* about the possibility of submarine attack. She warned Broussignac that if she were attacked she would immediately sink the *Gloire*. 'Do not worry,' signalled Broussignac. 'You are not obliged to stay with me. Let me return quietly to Casablanca, since I have given you my word to proceed there.'[6] The *Australia*, anxious in any case to rejoin Cunningham's force in readiness for the move on Dakar, accepted Broussignac's assurance and early on the 21st left her to sail northwards alone. Broussignac was as good as his word and reached Casablanca on the 24th September.

So ended the bizarre chase that had been for Cunningham nothing but a maddening diversion from his main purpose—the execution of Operation Menace. But it had turned out to be much more than that: a major reverse for the Vichy French. Admiral Bourrague's mission to ensure Vichy control of French Equatorial Africa had been frustrated. Of the assorted flotilla that had left Dakar on this mission between the 14th and 18th September—the tanker *Tarn* and the cruiser *Primauguet*, the cargo-boat *Poitiers*, and Bourrague's three cruisers—all but two vessels had been written off. One of them was sunk, and three were heading back to Casablanca. The remaining two, the cruisers *Georges Leygues* and *Montcalm*, were bottled up in Dakar, an unforeseen addition to the port's defences against Operation Menace admittedly, but useless for anything else. Whatever the outcome of Menace itself, the pursuit action forced on Cunningham had produced its own success.

This was plain from Vichy's swift reaction. The Vichy Government had pinned high hopes on the success of Bourrague's mission. On the afternoon of the 19th the French Admiralty cabled him at sea reiterating the importance of his task, at the very moment he was running into trouble with Cunningham's force. And Darlan was so angry to learn of the setback to Bourrague's squadron during the same night that he renewed his order—rescinded shortly before—to attack all British warships found within a 20-mile zone of the coast. But his heaviest wrath had fallen on Bourrague himself. Within hours of Bourrague's return to Dakar Darlan had fired off a cable to him relieving him of his command. And the general chagrin of the Vichy leaders at what they regarded as a lamentable fiasco was summed up by Paul Baudouin, France's Foreign Secretary, who recorded in his diary for the 20th September: 'We are going to appear fools in the eyes both of the Germans and the English!'[7]

In London, meanwhile, Churchill was remaining adamant about the necessity for taking Dakar—even at the cost of serious fighting. On the 22nd September he informed General Smuts: '. . . The de Gaulle movement to rescue the French colonies had prospered in Equatoria and the Cameroons. We could not allow these solid gains to be destroyed by French warships and personnel from Vichy, sent probably at German dictation. If Dakar fell under German control and became a U-boat base the consequences to the Cape Route would be deadly. We have therefore set out upon the business of putting de Gaulle into Dakar, peaceably if we can, forcibly if we must, and the expedition now about to strike seems to have the necessary force.

'Naturally the risk of a bloody collision with the French sailors and part of the garrison is not a light one. On the whole I think the odds are heavily against any serious resistance, having regard to the low morale and unhappy plight of this French colony . . . Still, no one can be sure till we try . . .'[8]

And next day he was to cable President Roosevelt: 'I was encouraged by your reception of information conveyed by Lord Lothian [British Ambassador to the US] about Dakar. It would be against our joint interests if strong German submarine and aircraft bases were established there. It looks as if there might be a stiff fight. Perhaps not, but orders have been given to ram it through . . .'[9]

For General Irwin, putting the last touches to his plans at Freetown—where his staff handed out 'sandbags of orders' to the Marines—the sortie of the Vichy cruisers from Dakar had brought its own troubles. When the *Devonshire* left port to head the chase, he had to move his headquarters to the transport *Karanja*. And next day he was to shift again, to the battleship *Barham*, to rejoin Cunningham when the admiral transferred his flag there from the *Devonshire* to lead the expedition into action. Here conditions for him and his staff were even worse than in the *Devonshire*. The heat was more infernal, the space still more restricted. The military office was right aft of the main deck, and soon after sailing for Dakar, that part of the ship was to be shut down to reduce the space liable to flooding if the ship were torpedoed. The staff were then crowded into the plotting room, and had practically to take over the admiral's bridge. Sleeping and eating arrangements were a penance whose full grimness would become apparent in the coming days of the operation.

Sailing date had been set back 48 hours by the French squadron's break-out; and now, at dawn on Sunday, 22nd September, the alarms and excursions over and the final dispositions made, the warships, transports and auxiliary vessels of Operation Menace edged out of Freetown harbour—destination Dakar.

On de Gaulle's headquarters ship, the *Westernland*, the Spears Mission now underwent final briefing. 'General Spears addressed the troops of the Mission,' recorded Mitchell. 'I took the parade. I accompanied the stern and silent General de Gaulle as he inspected the parade. General Spears explained to the officers that the movement might be the turning point in the war. If after landing we manage to link up with the French troops in North Africa, possibilities are tremendous.[10]

'That evening I was invited to a dinner party with General Spears, General de Gaulle and other officers, in a very stifling mess-room. As I was an old Tank Corps man of the 1914-1918 war I was seated next to General de Gaulle. On the table was a cake with the date in icing, "September 22nd", and ornamented with green and pink roses. We each had a piece. To hear the perfect, anecdotal, classical French of General Spears was an unexpected treat. General de Gaulle talked about his *chars* (tanks). He said that the French Army had 2,000 but over 1,000 were knocked out in the first battles.

'"What happened to the others, *mon général?*" I asked. "There are only twelve left." "Only twelve?" I repeated in amazement. "Yes, they are with us now!" Shortly after this General de Gaulle addressed the assembled company. He related the story of the meeting on the eve of the battle of Cambrai in 1917 when General Elles, the commander of the Tank Corps, told his senior officers: "Tomorrow decides our fate. We are looking over ground chosen by us. We either lose and the Tank Corps is finished or we win and will multiply exceedingly."

'There was a solemn pause. General de Gaulle looked round the table. "Gentlemen, that is our position"!'

In these last hours before the strike, feeling on the *Barham* and the *Westernland* was tense. What reception would they meet at Dakar? After all the frustrations, delays and diversions, could Operation Menace possibly succeed? Any advantage of surprise had plainly been lost. But this was immaterial if the authorities and people were friendly. If, however, de Gaulle's landing were opposed and shooting started, could resistance be effectively overcome? A hopeful pointer to the situation in Dakar now came from the *Ark Royal*. A reconnaissance plane from the aircraft carrier, flying over the port, had reported the *Richelieu* and the French cruisers still—surprisingly—with their awnings spread, and no signs of unusual activity elsewhere. To the Free French service men on the *Ark Royal* this caused no surprise. They were convinced that the French Air Force and the majority of the civilian population were on their side, and believed that the garrison would give in after a few token shots had been exchanged.[11]

De Gaulle was still hoping likewise, though by now he was taking a more sober view about the possibilities of a walk-over. But anyone in the Menace convoy who might think the Dakar operation was going to be easy was in for a shock. As the Allied armada headed for Dakar over calm seas on the 22nd September, it was sailing into a major confrontation.

CHAPTER VIII

WILL DAKAR FIGHT?

Even Churchill had come round to thinking Dakar might fall fairly easily. As late as the 22nd he was telling Smuts that, despite the risk of a 'bloody collision,' the low morale of the population made serious resistance unlikely. But all the rosy Intelligence reports, all the forecasts of Dakar's quick and willing capitulation were to prove disastrously ill-founded. The population's low morale, if this meant hostility to Vichy, would not stop a single gun firing. And the Gaullist support within the town, on which so much faith had been based, was for all practical purposes non-existent. What counted was the attitude, and the power, of the civil authorities and armed forces. And these, whether or not they were specifically pro-Vichy, were—the sailors in particular—almost solidly hostile to de Gaulle and the British. Between them they had control of the town and the military resources to resist any but the heaviest outside attack. In short, anyone attempting to alter Dakar's status quo would do so at his peril.

In a string of forts commanding the approaches to Dakar harbour were seven coastal batteries mounting 18 guns of various calibres from heavy to light—Yoff, Mamelles, Cap Manuel, Gorée (two batteries), Bel Air and Rufisque. Two of these were manned by French Marines, the others by Senegalese gunners. In addition were a number of AA batteries. Supporting this first line of defence was a garrison of native troops including machine-gunners, commanded by French officers. And berthed in the boom-protected harbour was a formidable naval force: the 35,000-ton *Richelieu* with its 15-inch guns, the two Vichy cruisers *Georges Leygues* and *Montcalm* and their accompanying destroyers *Fantasque*, *Audacieux* and *Malin*, the destroyer *Hardi* and three submarines *Beveziers*, *Persée* and *Ajax*. Smaller craft included half-a-dozen sloops, three patrol boats, a tanker and sundry auxiliary vessels. Of aircraft, one Curtiss fighter group was based at nearby Ouakam airfield, and a bomber group of Glenn Martins at Thiès. The importance of Dakar as a military and naval centre was measured by the bevy of high service chiefs stationed there: General Barrau, C-in-C, French West and Equatorial Africa; General Arnoux, commanding Senegalese troops; General Picart, Defence Commander; General Gama, C-in-C, French West African Air Forces; Vice-Admiral Lacroix, commanding the Vichy squadron (in place of Admiral Bourrague); and Admiral Landriau, C-in-C French Naval Forces in French West and Equatorial Africa, and the Naval Division in French West Africa.[1]

Apart from de Gaulle's departure from England, reported on the 8th September (which may or may not have been seen at Dakar as a threat to West Africa), there had been plenty to alert the authorities to the possibility of an Allied attempt in recent days. There were the tortuous manoeuvrings of Bourrague's warships since their passage of the Straits on the 11th, the presence of British warships in the area, and the arrival of the massive Allied convoy at Freetown. And intelligence reaching Dakar from rumour-ridden Freetown and elsewhere had been evidence enough that some operation against the base was imminent. An attack had been expected first on the 17th, then on the 22nd. Yet as late as the 22nd there was doubt in Dakar as to what form the coming operation would take.

Two service chiefs thought the port might be blockaded rather than attacked. One was Admiral Landriau, and the other Admiral Lacroix, the dismissed Bourrague's newly-arrived successor. Lacroix, commanding the 3rd Cruiser Squadron at Toulon, had been flown to Dakar at a moment's notice on the 21st, with the barest briefing and bringing with him just a travelling case. Hastily reviewing the situation with Landriau on the morning of the 22nd, late that afternoon he joined Landriau in sending a long cable to the French Admiralty. All in all it was not encouraging for Vichy.

'Restoration order in disaffected area impossible with our present resources . . .' it ran. 'We have arrived too late. Latest events show that English are determined to use force to stop us putting down the rebels in French Equatorial Africa . . . Impossible to oppose them with our present surface ships without risking new humiliations for our crews or formal breaking out of hostilities . . . The English ultimatum gives impression that any force assembled at Dakar not favoured by British. Logically this must lead either to blockade or attack on Dakar . . . For the moment attack seems risky. On other hand blockade possible and leads to complete strangling French West Africa. This blockade can only be accelerated by hostile act or disloyal attitude on our part. I estimate, given our resources, that only solution is, on the governmental level, to establish with the British an agreement, tacit at least, allowing passage transports as provided for in personnel and revictualling—vital matter for us—and to do everything to avoid open hostilities between France and England.'[2]

Things had changed greatly in Dakar since the fall of France three months before. Then this spacious colonial city 15 degrees north of the equator on the peninsula of Cape Verde, fanned by ocean breezes, with its broad palm-lined avenues and bustling business streets, its colourful market, fine public buildings, imposing Roman Catholic cathedral and Governor's Palace conspicuous on its bluff above the bay (Dakar had been the capital of the colony of French West Africa for nearly 40 years) had known none of the realities of war. Housing a population of some 15,000 whites and 90,000 Africans, most of these living in the primitive overcrowded Medina quarter, it still retained much of its peacetime character as a great port and commercial centre, a place of call for trans-Atlantic shipping, and traffic from Europe to points around Africa, an important bunkering station, an entrepot for the prosperous African ground-nut trade. The chief reminders of Dakar's strategic significance for the French were the powerful forts on the island of Gorée, just outside the harbour, and those commanding the harbour's entrance on Cap Manuel.

Remote as were the Dakar colonists from the war in Europe, their immediate reaction to France's defeat was to rally to their fallen Motherland. On 20th June, two days after de Gaulle had launched from London his first call for continued resistance, 2,000 Europeans had gathered before Dakar's Memorial to the Dead and sworn to carry on the fight beside Britain. In the following days Frenchmen went in their hundreds, officials, servicemen, settlers, to the British Consulate seeking to enrol in the British forces or the newly-formed Free French movement of de Gaulle. It was an instinctive realization by these colonists that the vast untouched resources of the French Empire should be thrown into the balance against Germany.

According to a senior colonial official, M. Beretta, who was at Dakar from the time of the armistice until the beginning of August (when he was banished to Dahomey on account of his Free French sympathies), it was Dakar's example that inspired the spirit of resistance in France's other West African colonies. And the Vichy Government, noting the potential danger, had moved swiftly to counter it by sending to Dakar early in July the experienced colonial administrator, Pierre Boisson. Boisson held the double appointment of High Commissioner for French West Africa and Governor-General of Dakar. A tough forceful Breton in his mid-forties, he was a First World War veteran who had lost a leg at Verdun and who also suffered from partial deafness. But, making light of these disabilities, he was known for his clarity of mind and dynamic energy. He would stump up steep hills without the aid of a stick, and at the end of a long day at his desk would mount his horse for a strenuous gallop.

In these uneasy weeks at Dakar, Boisson faced a delicate

situation. As a loyal French patriot he wanted above all to see the downfall of Germany and the preservation of the French Empire. He was violently opposed to anything that seemed to work against these ends. As he saw it, support for the Free French movement or the British was a sure way to invite German intervention in Africa with consequent grave danger to the integrity of France's imperial possessions. He was therefore determined to suppress any Gaullist sympathies among the people of Dakar. In his view the Empire's true interests lay quite elsewhere. 'I had one anxiety,' he was to tell a friend in September, 'this was to maintain French prestige in the eyes of the natives. They knew sure enough that France had been defeated, but so long as nothing in West Africa had changed for them, it was possible that the effect of this defeat, which I hoped would be temporary, would be minimized. It had taken place a long way away from them. But the presence of the Germans would have brought it right home to them. And of course, their presence would have been accompanied by German propaganda which, as is everywhere the case, would have gained support.'[3]

Boisson had shown his aims even before arriving at Dakar. At the end of June he had formed a plan to create an 'African block' aimed at strengthening and preserving the independence of the Empire. He had cabled the North African Governors asking them to keep contact and exchange information but had received no reply. On the 26th he had broadcast a speech from Brazzaville advocating imperial solidarity. 'The safety of France does not lie in the dispersal of its overseas strength,' he said. 'It lies in standing together.' And on the 6th July he had broadcast again, declaring: 'Our duty is to preserve and defend what has been entrusted to us.'[4] But if his plan came to nothing, at least he was determined, on taking over at Dakar, to see that Dakar itself was not seduced from its patriotic loyalties.

Boisson was already well known and liked at Dakar, and his arrival there acted to steady a population perplexed and uncertain about the future. His first radio address, and his announcement of various economic and financial measures, helped to restore confidence; as did his assurance that none of the armistice clauses signed by France affected her colonial Empire, and that no German or Italian would set foot in Africa. And soon, as the disrupted air traffic with France was restored and mail, newspapers and even goods began arriving again, life was returning to a semblance of normal. Meanwhile Boisson set about instituting a series of reforms in agricultural, forestry and other spheres aimed at increasing the country's prosperity and even supplying the pressing needs of the Motherland. In short, in these weeks he was doing everything possible to keep the war and its effects away from West Africa, so that here at least France's defeat would not be felt and some of her imperial assets preserved.

But just before Boisson's arrival, Dakar had been reminded that it was not immune from war. On the 8th July, on a follow-up operation to the Royal Navy's shattering assault on the French fleet at Mers-el-Kebir five days before (Operation Catapult), the British launched an attack on the battleship *Richelieu* in Dakar harbour. The 35,000-ton *Richelieu*, one of France's newest warships, had escaped from Brest shortly before the armistice and arrived at Dakar on the 24th June. So long as she remained at this strategic Atlantic port she could, if coming under German control, constitute a grave threat to British shipping on the Cape route. It was therefore decided to offer her terms for leaving Dakar, with the alternative of being attacked and sunk. On the 7th July a British force arrived off Dakar and presented the ultimatum, which gave the *Richelieu* the choice of being conducted to England or the Antilles, being disarmed, or scuttling herself. No reply was received, and early on the 8th the attack went in.

A motor-boat from the aircraft-carrier *Hermes* got through the defences and placed depth-charges under the *Richelieu*'s stern to cripple her rudders and propellors. But owing to the shallowness of the water these failed to explode; and soon after, six torpedo-bombers from the *Hermes* attacked, scoring one hit which twisted a propellor shaft and flooded three compartments. The damage, though not vital, was to take a year to repair. In immobilizing this powerful warship which might have been a valuable asset to the enemy, the attack was a success. But among Frenchmen at Dakar this unprovoked onslaught caused deep shock and anger. It strengthened still further the anti-British (and anti-Gaullist) feeling aroused by the Mers-el-Kebir attack.

The toughest anti-British mood was likely to be found among the sailors at Dakar, comrades of the Mers-el-Kebir victims. Which makes all the stranger the story that appeared a few months later in an African French-language paper.[5] It was reported that when the *Richelieu* was attacked, her commander, Admiral Laborde, ordered her and her two accompanying destroyers to open fire on the British, and that 800 of their crews refused. They would not fight against their recent allies, beside whom many of them had campaigned at Narvik and Dunkirk. Thereupon Laborde had them disembarked and sent to a camp in the interior of Senegal. Their treatment provoked such anger among their fellows that they were moved back to Dakar and shipped to France in the liner *Ville d'Algers*. Laborde, a convinced Anglophobe, was so furious that he decided to carry out a reprisal raid on Britain's neighbouring Gambia territory. When he asked for volunteers, six men came forward and the plan was dropped.

The source of this report was the pro-Gaullist colonial official Beretta, who was in Dakar at the time. True or untrue, blatant exaggeration or piece of wishful thinking, it typified the anti-Vichy propaganda then being put around by Gaullist supporters. Much of this was directed against Boisson himself, allegedly so pro-Vichy and pro-German. One story described Boisson's shabby treatment of a senior colonial administrator, M. Louveau, whose loyalty to de Gaulle he was aware of. Meeting Louveau in early July on his way to assume his post at Dakar, Boisson told him that he understood his attitude, but that he (Boisson) would take up no definite position about de Gaulle until he reached Dakar. He added, pointing to his artificial leg: 'You see this. It was the Germans who were responsible.' Shortly afterwards he called Louveau to Dakar and had him locked up in the town's noisome Medina jail. But his lost leg, it was said, did not stop him dining with members of a visiting German Commission.[6]

Boisson's alleged reception at Dakar of a German Armistice Commission was one of the main Gaullist charges against him. The presence of Germans at Dakar—which could be interpreted as a first step towards the enemy's occupation of West Africa— made useful ammunition for anyone anxious to discredit Boisson and the Vichy Government. The British themselves were to use it when, during the chase of Bourrague's cruisers by Cunningham's force on 19th September, the *Georges Leygius* was told not to enter Dakar which was 'under German control.' The Ministry of Information was to use it, too, to justify Operation Menace. And de Gaulle was to underline the German peril by stating in a communiqué to the public about Dakar, after the failure of Menace, that the Germans were proposing to occupy the port.

There was in fact nothing in the German Armistice Commission tale, nor were the Germans then planning to occupy Dakar. But in a city rife with rumour and speculation, almost anything could be believed. According to one report, at the end of July four German planes landed at Dakar's airfield bringing the Commission, whose members were received by Colonel Herckel, Chief of Staff to the C-in-C, General Barrau. The Germans were accommodated in official premises and took their meals in the Hotel Metropole. Here they were said to have been seen of an evening, quaffing champagne in the company of Herckel and Police Commissioner Kieffer, who was in charge of their security.[7]

The 'villain' of the Commission myth was a German called Dr Klaube. Klaube, a former director of the German airways line, Lufthansa, at Bathurst, capital of the Gambia, was supposed to be the head of an undercover German Mission at Dakar, working as a fifth column with the connivance of Boisson. He had arrived at Dakar early in July with two naval officers and other Germans, it was alleged, all of whom knew West Africa intimately. To maintain secrecy they discarded their uniforms—Klaube was now apparently an army colonel—and while some of them returned shortly to North Africa, Klaube continued his activities in civilian guise, getting information, making trips to Morocco to report to his chiefs, organizing spy networks, travelling everywhere he wanted and bringing other German agents in, furnished with Swiss, Swedish or Belgian passports. Klaube was careful to avoid direct contact with his colleagues, and recruited minor agents from hangers-on around the port.

But the truth about Dr Klaube was in reality very different. As well as being a Lufthansa director, he was before the war a consular agent at Bathurst, being also well-known and popular at Dakar, which he often visited. After the outbreak of war Klaube had returned to Germany. Then in July 1940 Boisson was informed by Vichy's Minister for the Colonies that he was to receive a German 'diplomat'—namely Dr Klaube—who was charged with arranging the repatriation, under the terms of the armistice, of the 100 or so German subjects, mostly the crews of scuttled or torpedoed merchant ships, who had been interned in a local camp since September 1939. Klaube arrived by transport plane at Ouakam airport, Dakar, on 27th July, alone except for a small repatriation unit. He was met at the airport by the Chief of the *Sûreté*. The repatriation arrangements went ahead, and the plane took off with its first batch of internees. Meanwhile Klaube remained at Dakar, being permitted to renew contacts with various pre-war friends—but always closely accompanied by Police Commissioner Kieffer. It was because Kieffer, who came from Alsace, spoke fluent German that rumours started that two Germans were moving freely around Dakar. And other unfounded suspicions were aroused by further incidents. On its second trip the repatriation plane brought in a badly wounded German flying ace and a young naval lieutenant. The latter, it seemed, did wish to examine the lay-out of the local defences, but immediately this became known he was packed off with his companion on the aircraft's next flight, with no harm done. There was a further tale about a German inspecting Dakar's coast batteries. But this too was false. The

'German' turned out to be Colonel Herckel who, being an Alsatian like Police Commissioner Kieffer, spoke French with a guttural accent. As for Dr Klaube, he left Dakar for good on the last flight of the repatriation plane on 3rd August.

If London was taking the rumours about Germans at Dakar seriously, they were also causing concern across the Atlantic. The United States Government had been anxiously watching the course of events in Africa since the fall of France. Now, at the end of July, the State Department in its turn received information that a German delegation of naval and air force technical experts and harbour engineers had arrived at Dakar to make a survey of the port's military installations. In view of the threat German occupation of Dakar would pose for the United States, this report was sufficient to spur the Government to action. It was thought essential to have an American on the spot to watch and report on developments. At this time there was no American consulate at Dakar, the post having been closed on economy grounds ten years before. So now it was decided to reopen the post, and on 6th August an experienced consular official, Thomas C. Wesson, was appointed to Dakar.

Wesson arrived at Dakar on the 14th September—the day that Bourrague's squadron slipped out of Casablanca southward bound, and the first of the Allied convoy reached Freetown. His arrival was quiet and informal. He presented his credentials to the gendarmes at the pier, called on Boisson, whom he found 'hospitable', and next day hoisted his consular flag above the US consulate. From then on, aided by a large staff, he was to keep a sharp and watchful eye on the build-up of events in Dakar at this time of growing tension, and eight days later was to witness the Operation Menace attempt. And he was in a first-rate position to know of the presence at Dakar of any Germans. What he was afterwards to testify about this is significant. While he was unable to confirm or deny the truth about the technical delegation's visit from personal knowledge, his general findings strongly suggest that this was even more far-fetched than the other stories.

Wesson was to state that during his time as consul at Dakar
there were—except for a few Jewish refugees—no Germans
there, nor any German activities. Furthermore, no German
ships or submarines called at Dakar or other West African ports,
and no locally-based warship left port to revictual any German
vessels. In a country predominantly of black men, any white
stranger or newcomer would, he said, easily have been picked
out. And seeing that, with a few exceptions, the whole white
population hated the Germans, news of their arrival in French
West Africa would have flashed quickly round the community.
Even if a German had landed secretly by plane or submarine,
at his listening-post in the consulate Wesson would certainly
have heard about it. Likewise he would have known if officers
and crews of Dakar-based warships had had any contacts with
Germans while at sea: news of this would surely have got
around when the Frenchmen came on shore leave after returning to port.

Wesson conceded that, before his own arrival, Dr Klaube
had visited Dakar to repatriate the German internees, but had
left early in August. Citing the evidence of official records, he
was to assert that during his stay in Dakar the Germans frequently pressed the Vichy Government for permission to send
German missions to Dakar, but this was always strongly opposed
by Boisson—who on one occasion travelled to Vichy to make
his objections personally. Indeed, it may well have been
Boisson's intransigence that prevented the Germans from coming
to Dakar. 'From my observations,' Wesson was to conclude, 'I
should say that Boisson has shown himself a capable colonial
administrator, honest, impetuous and efficient. Two domi-
nating aims have guided him during my stay at Dakar: in-
flexible opposition to any foreign attempt against French
sovereignty or to any foreign attempt to undermine the authority of the French State in the regions under his jurisdiction.'[8]

In Wesson's judgement, Boisson was clearly determined to
keep any intruder out of Dakar, whether Free French, British or
German. And ironically, at the very moment that the Allied

convoy was en route to carry out Operation Menace, the French were being assured that the British for their part had no intention of interfering in France's African territories. On 12th September Paul Baudouin, Vichy's Foreign Minister, received a telegram from his Ambassador to Spain, M. de la Baume, reporting a talk with his British counterpart in Madrid, Sir Samuel Hoare. 'The British Ambassador,' Baudouin noted, 'would seem to appreciate that it is to his country's interests as well as our own to maintain the status quo in French North and West Africa. His Government, he said, ". . . does not wish to take any steps which might embroil the two countries." I stressed once more the fundamental problem, and said [presumably in reply to Baume]: "If once British propaganda arouses alarm in Berlin, Rome, or Madrid that our colonies are going over to de Gaulle and are going to be sued by Great Britain, nothing will stop Germany, Italy, and Spain from taking steps to prevent any such development".'[9]

But what of France's own determination to defend her colonies? This was a vital matter for the Germans, and they were anxious for reassurance on it. Two days later the German Ambassador to Vichy, Herr Abetz, questioned Baudouin about the situation in Africa. Baudouin declared that the French were determined to face all opponents, whoever they might be, and outlined the defence measures that had been organized at Casablanca and Dakar. Abetz replied that it was a pity that the armistice had not provided for the occupation of North Africa, as Germany lacked the security which this would have afforded. 'I informed him,' recorded Baudouin, 'that the German Great General Staff ought to know that if it had put forward this demand the French Government would not have signed the armistice.'[10]

So, with Britain deceitfully assuring Vichy France of her pacific intentions regarding Africa, and France—anxious to believe Britain but taking no chances anyway—assuring Germany that she was able and determined to defend her colonies, Dakar had become a pawn in a minor game of power politics. The coming Allied attempt to win it over could provoke grave consequences for everyone involved. Britain might find herself at war with France, and France might suffer the occupation of her African colonies by Germany. As the unfortunate figure in the middle, all that Boisson could do was protect this bone of contention against all comers.

After urgent preparation, by September's third week Dakar was ready to meet attack. Inter-service liaison had been tightened, the native garrison alerted and reservists called-up, routine reconnaissance flights instituted as well as sea patrols covering a 25-mile radius of the port. Two anti-invasion exercises were carried out, and coast artillery defences overhauled. In the harbour the *Richelieu* and the two Toulon cruisers along with other vessels and submarines were standing by for action. (The *Richelieu*'s spread awnings, as spotted by the *Ark Royal*'s planes on the 22nd, could only give false hopes to those optimists who thought her 15-inch guns were not ready to fire on intruders.) To refute Churchill's suggestion of fairly massive reinforcements brought by Bourrague's warships to Dakar, the only additional force landed there by Bourrague was a contingent of 120 coast gunners. These took over two batteries at Cap Manuel and Bel Air, previously manned by crews from the *Richelieu*, who now returned to their ship. There had been some recent reinforcement of aircraft, and as previously mentioned there was one group of Curtiss fighters stationed at the somewhat cramped airfield of Ouakam, four miles from Dakar.

In the town and port, the belief that some Allied move was imminent had steadily grown. There was common talk that Dakar would be the first place in French West Africa to be 'liberated' by Anglo-French forces. On the many neutral and other merchant ships immobilized in Dakar harbour speculation buzzed about what would happen if the Allies attacked. The local garrison was not considered formidable, though it was recognized that the guns of the *Richelieu* could deal out devastating damage. On the 14th, the sight of Bourrague's squadron as it first appeared on the horizon caused great excitement among the Norwegian vessels. Elated seamen asked each other if the Allies had come at last. Then, when it was clear that the warships were French, despondency took over. To dejected Norwegians—whose country lay under the Nazi yoke—it seemed impossible that an Allied attack on Dakar could succeed in the face of these Vichy reinforcements. The departure of the cruisers four days later brought these Scandinavians no cheer. If Vichy warships could sail so freely along the important sea-lanes off the African coast, the British Navy must be in a poor way, they thought.

And, in the cafés, back rooms and private meeting-places of Dakar, what of the Free French sympathizers on whose help de Gaulle had been so much relying? Since Boisson's arrival the fervid, open support for de Gaulle that had marked the first days after France's defeat had been virtually silenced. The backing was still there beneath the surface, but it was ineffectual, unorganized and without leadership. When it did emerge it was vigorously dealt with by the authorities. Notable was the example of M. Kaouza, director of Dakar's *Ecole Normale*. At the time of the armistice Kaouza was serving in the French forces in the Sudan. Staggered by France's defeat, he determined to join the resistance. In July, after demobilization, he arrived back at Dakar and contacted fellow-sympathizers, among whom were the Mayor of Dakar and the President of the Chamber of Commerce. The meetings continued through August, but to no practical effect. Then, in September, Kaouza left Dakar on the pretext of a hunting trip and reached Bathurst in the Gambia. Here he visited the British Governor, declaring his Gaullist sympathies and asking him to communicate with de Gaulle in London. The Governor did so, passing on Kaouza's appeal that any operation to be mounted at Dakar must be by Frenchmen. Kaouza then got a Bathurst printing-press to run off a quantity of tracts calling on Dakar's citizens to follow de Gaulle. On 5th September he left by canoe to return to Dakar, accompanied by a native who concealed the tracts under his ample robe. But Kaouza's effort met with failure. On reaching French territory he was immediately arrested, escorted under strong guard to Dakar, taken to the

Sûreté headquarters and jailed.

Another resistance effort had been mounted by a local administrator named Bissagnet. Working from the Senegal town of Foundiougne and aided by a colleague named Campistron, Bissagnet formed contacts with native leaders sympathetic to de Gaulle. He also organized a surveillance network to monitor the anti-Gaullist activities allegedly set up by Boisson in the nearby Gambia territories. Associated with Bissagnet and Campistron was a naval officer, de Mersuey, who managed to get to Dakar, where he collected information on local service morale and defence plans. The operations of this group extended to points around Dakar, St Louis and Rufisque, where they apparently found Gaullist support among the garrisons. Then on 17th September two Free French officers appeared at Foundiougne with the momentous news of the forthcoming Allied operation against Dakar. This was taken as the moment to alert Gaullist supporters over the whole area, and warning messages went out from Kaolack, where some of the group were based, to points in Senegal, the Sudan and Nigeria. These scattered units of loyalists were, it seemed, only awaiting a successful coup by de Gaulle himself to raise the Free French standard far and wide throughout Africa.

At Dakar itself, as defence preparations went ahead, anti-Gaullist measures were intensified. The actual strength of Gaullist support at this time is hard to determine. Members of the Norwegian crews who met French officers and civilians ashore found that many favoured de Gaulle but were not advertising their views. And they gained the impression that the Dakar forces would not offer de Gaulle serious resistance if he attempted to land. Alongside the Gaullists and the Vichyites there was a considerable body of neutral opinion. An officer of the French submarine *Ajax* which arrived at Dakar from Casablanca on the 20th estimated neutrals—people who were indifferent or who wanted to avoid trouble—as 50%, with Gaullist supporters at 20% and Vichyites at 30%.[11] Earlier the Gaullist sympathiser Kaouza, in his message to de Gaulle, had put Gaullists at 40%, Vichyites (notably including naval units) at

20%, with the undecided or indifferent at 40%.[12]

But a later report from Kaouza—dated 18th September—
showed a notable shift to de Gaulle. Whether Kaouza was still
in jail on the 18th, or how he got his report out—and even
whether de Gaulle received it—is uncertain. But what he said
was: 'Sixty per cent of the population share your views. The
military are divided, whereas the Navy is rather hostile. The
coastal batteries and the colonial infantry are rather hesitant.
On the whole people think selfishly and everybody thinks of their
own particular interests. It is at present a panicky country. The
civil servants are afraid of losing their jobs. However, the ex-
servicemen, business people, the working classes, certain groups
of officials are ready to help the cause and declare their opinions
openly.' Significantly, Kaouza added: 'The naval quarters are
infested with machine-gun posts fronting towards the town, that
is against the civil population. The people are grumbling.'[13]

In terms of practical Gaullist support, this was not encouraging. Now, on the eve of the launching of Menace, de Gaulle's
best hope—and this seemed pretty forlorn—of mobilizing his
followers into any kind of effective force lay in his emissary,
dispatched from Freetown on the 16th, Boislambert.

After a hazardous journey, Boislambert had reached
Foundiougne with a companion on the evening of the 20th.
Thence, by devious moves, he reached Dakar early on the 22nd,
accompanied by Bissagnet whom he had contacted at Foundiougne. At Dakar the two were given shelter by a Gaullist
friend of Bissagnet, who briefed them on the sabotage work
they were to carry out on the service telephone lines and cables.
That afternoon they went out by bicycle, noting the location
of their targets and taking stock of the various military installations. The town was quiet and everything seemed normal.
The sailors from the cruisers were strolling in the streets and
sitting in the cafés, glad that they had been granted shore leave
—as they were heard to say—until midnight. Nobody took
special notice of the two men as they cycled leisurely about the
town in the hot afternoon.

In the evening they were joined by the naval officer, de

Mersuey, who had arrived by train from Kaolack, and with him contacted various civilian and military supporters. Then, late that night, they prepared to go into action. Changing from their white drill into less conspicuous khaki, they made rendezvous with a group of local resisters who had brought with them an armament of pliers, chisels and iron bars for the sabotage work. What they had set out to do seemed incredibly risky. To get at the wires and cables, they had to drive holes into the pavement at prearranged places, with no means of masking the noise. Boislambert's particular task was to destroy, with the aid of one helper, the switchboard of the naval arsenal at nearby Hann. The various operations took the whole night, and some were still going on as dawn broke on the 23rd and early risers appeared on the streets. But, almost miraculously, nowhere were the saboteurs detected. In a few hectic hours—in their race to pave the way for the Anglo-French armada which was now almost within sight of Dakar—they had cut the telephone cable linking Bel Air radio station and Naval HQ, the telephone connections with the Cap Manuel battery, and the Dakar–Thiès railway line.

CHAPTER IX

MENACE DAY ONE—
THE PLAN MISFIRES

Around dawn on Monday 23rd September Dakar was aroused by the roar of planes flying low over the town and the crash of anti-aircraft fire from the harbour. People who were abroad early and others who ran to look out of their windows were astonished to see streams of paper fluttering down on the streets and quays, and into the harbour—a bombardment of tricolour leaflets bearing a boldly printed message. Those who picked them up read: 'I, General de Gaulle, come to bring you food and tell you to join with me to continue the struggle. We come to defend Dakar with you. We come to ensure the food supplies of Dakar—General de Gaulle.' Another leaflet proclaimed: 'Dakar is threatened by the enemy and by famine! Dakar must be preserved for France. It is for this that French forces have come to Dakar under my orders . . . I invite the people to be calm and show their patriotism and give a welcome to my soldiers! Long live French Africa! *Vive la France!* General de Gaulle.'

With this dramatic overture from the skies—carried out by four Swordfish planes from the aircraft carrier *Ark Royal*—Operation Menace had begun.

Almost simultaneously the other opening stroke of Menace was under way. Two small Luciole planes, also from the *Ark Royal*, were landing at nearby Ouakam airfield with four Free French officers who would pave the way for the later landing by boat of de Gaulle's envoys. Since soon after 4 am activity on the *Ark Royal* had been intense, for she was responsible for the preliminary phase of Operation Menace. Preparing for take-off from her dimly lit flight-deck had been a succession of planes on various missions. Besides the leaflet-dropping Swordfish and the Lucioles, other Swordfish were detailed as follows: one to observe and report on the Ouakam landing, four to take additional Free French personnel to Ouakam (if the first landing was successful), two to carry out reconnaissance, two to maintain an anti-submarine patrol. There were anxious moments as the Lucioles took off, for the two Free French pilots had no night flying experience, had never flown a Luciole nor flown off a carrier. But somehow both managed to get airborne and away without mishap.

As the Allied convoy had approached Dakar before dawn, weather conditions had been good, with clear skies, bright moonlight and a calm sea. Only one thing was wrong: a thick surface mist that reduced visibility to two miles. To watchers on the *Westernland* and other ships this was disquieting. On the voyage to Freetown, de Gaulle and his staff had closely studied the weather records for the Dakar region in late September and had been assured of ideal conditions, including unlimited visibility. Now this unexpected mist raised the uneasy query: would it lift with the coming of daylight, or would it persist—or get worse? Good visibility was absolutely essential for the operation. The Anglo-French armada had to be seen, its assembled strength an added inducement—if that were needed—for Dakar to accept de Gaulle. As yet the mist was the mere shadow of a threat. A freshening wind could shift it or the quickly mounting sun could burn it off. Meanwhile the first stage of Menace must go ahead as planned.

By dawn the convoy had reached its rendezvous off Dakar. Cruising slowly to and fro in a strung-out line, it was a fearsome-looking force: the two battleships *Barham* and *Resolution*; the aircraft carrier *Ark Royal*; the heavy cruisers *Devonshire*, *Australia*, *Cumberland*; the light cruiser *Delhi*; the ten destroyers including *Fortune*, *Foresight*, *Greyhound*, *Inglefield*, *Fury*, *Faulkner*,

Dragon; the two patrol boats *Milford* and *Bridgewater*; the three French sloops *Savorgnan de Brazza*, *Commandant Duboc*, *Commandant Dominé*; and the two armed trawlers *President Houduce* and *Vaillant*. Closer inshore, bulked the transports *Ettrick*, *Kenya*, *Karanja*, *Sobieski*, *Westernland* and *Pennland*, carrying between them some 7,000 British and Free French troops. With them sailed the supply vessels *Belgravia*, *Anadyr*, *Fort-Lamy* and *Casamance*. Of aircraft the *Ark Royal* carried 16 Swordfish and 16 Skua fighters, and the British warships six Walrus planes. Appearing on a clear and sunlit dawn horizon, such a massed array might well have struck fear into watchers who spotted it from Dakar's look-out posts. But unfortunately for the Allied convoy, the persistent wall of haze made it invisible from the shore.

The British battleship strength was, however, not as formidable as it appeared. The *Resolution* and the *Barham* both carried eight 15-inch and 12 6-inch guns, and the *Resolution*, completed in 1916, was fully efficient and capable of 20 knots. But the *Barham*, completed in 1915 and partially modernized, with a speed of 24 knots, was just re-commissioned and her new crew had had no battle practice. This deficiency would be crucial in the coming operation.

The tract-dropping planes and the Lucioles had gone in under a mist that, if anything, was thickening. But some 30 minutes after the Lucioles' departure good news had come back to the *Ark Royal*. The Free French had entered the hangars and emerged to spread on the ground the pre-arranged strips announcing 'Success.' Anticipating this signal, the first of the four other Ouakam-bound Swordfish had already taken off, and now the rest followed. But hardly had the first landed when the patrolling Swordfish reported French fighters taking the air. Seconds later fire was opened from the ground, and then the spotter plane reported the three remaining Swordfish heading back out to sea, hotly pursued by the fighters. Displayed outside Ouakam's hangars still lay the ground-strips ironically proclaiming 'Success,' but the failure of the mission was obvious. From the *Ark Royal* to Cunningham's flagship, the *Barham*, went the laconic report: 'All aircraft recalled. Further departures cancelled.'

The Free French had landed at Ouakam just as the airfield personnel were parading for morning duty. The officer in command, Commandant de la Horie, immediately challenged them and was seized and bound while his men stood by, too astonished to move. This apparently had led the Free French to think the whole thing was a walk-over; hence the premature registering of 'Success.' But de la Horie's shouts brought another officer on the scene who, arming himself with a machine-gun and calling on some nearby airmen, quickly freed the commandant and captured and tied up the attackers. The miscarriage of the move on Ouakam was serious. It meant that not only were de Gaulle's men denied the hoped-for use of the airfield, but also that the follow-up Free French airmen were unable to land and carry out their own vital mission—the commandeering of transport which they would drive to the port to meet the Free French emissaries who were shortly arriving there by launch.

These emissaries—the men who, led by Commandant Thierry d'Argenlieu, were to present letters from de Gaulle to Boisson and the army and naval chiefs—were already on their way. They had left the main force at 5.30 am in the sloop *Savorgnan de Brazza*, and 30 minutes later put off from her in two launches, the first carrying d'Argenlieu and fellow-envoys, the second a security crew. Both launches flew large tricolours and white truce flags and all the envoys were unarmed. Their arrival was not to be unannounced. As they edged forward to the now fog-bound port, from the *Westernland* de Gaulle was sending a radio message to Boisson: 'General de Gaulle comes with his troops to reinforce the defences of Dakar and to re-provision the town. A powerful English squadron and numerous British troops are here to support him. General de Gaulle has just sent officers of his staff to the authorities of Dakar. . . This delegation is commissioned to ask for the free disembarkation of French troops and of provisions. If all goes well, the British forces will not have to intervene and will not disembark. All the officers, soldiers, sailors, airmen and inhabitants of Dakar should strive to assist this work of salvation. General de Gaulle.'[1]

The two white-flagged launches after safely passing under the guns of Gorée Island, slipped past the long breakwaters and berthed at one of the quays just before 7 am. But immediately d'Argenlieu and his party had landed they were challenged by an officer brandishing a revolver.[2] Another rather friendlier officer then appeared, and d'Argenlieu informed him that he had letters to deliver to the High Commissioner and service chiefs. He refused a request to hand them over and insisted on delivering them personally. There was a brief parley as d'Argenlieu explained the situation to the chief of the Harbour Police, Commander Lorfèvre, and his deputy. Uncertain how to act, Lorfevre telephoned Admiral Landriau at Naval Headquarters and then sent an officer to him for instructions. While Landriau's orders were awaited, the group stood awkwardly about on the quay, attended by Lorfèvre. D'Argenlieu broke the strained silence by remarking to Lorfèvre that he had a fine fleet in the harbour. 'Yes,' replied Lorfèvre, 'it's ready to defend itself.' The exchange continued, then d'Argenlieu said: 'Our duty was to fulfil our obligations to England.' 'I obey my legitimate leaders,' retorted Lorfèvre. 'Our leaders have betrayed us,' was d'Argenlieu's answer.*

Meanwhile the officer had reported to Admiral Landriau. Landriau, having seen some of the Gaullist tracts, had already sized up the situation and alerted the Navy. He was now inclined to dismiss the story of the envoys as a bluff, and suspecting that their arrival might be linked with an internal fifth-column plot, immediately ordered their arrest. Back on the quay Lorfèvre received the order and told d'Argenlieu—somewhat apologetically—that he and his party were to be held. But he seemed in no hurry to act. D'Argenlieu, declaring that nobody was going to arrest him, made to get back into the launch with his companions. At this point the officer who had threatened them with his revolver dashed along the quay and

---

* Versions differ about what happened on the quay and immediately afterwards, but this account is compiled largely from d'Argenlieu's own story, with additions from others that seem to fit in with it.

ordered a nearby machine-gunner to open fire on it as it was moving off. What happened next is uncertain. The machine-gunner was apparently ordered to stop firing after loosing a few ineffective rounds. Then, when the two launches, pursued by the tugboat *Ouakam*, had gained some distance across the harbour, more shots rang out either from the *Richelieu*, berthed not far off, or from a battery on Gorée Island. A stream of bullets crashed into d'Argenlieu's launch, wounding him and a companion, Captain Perrin. The two launches chugged on towards the mist-bound open sea, in humiliating retreat, to be joined by the *Savorgnan de Brazza*, which awaited them outside the harbour entrance.

On the Norwegian merchantman *Lidvard*, in Dakar harbour, the dawn sound of planes over the town had caused little interest. But when leaflets started showering on her decks, announcing the coming of de Gaulle, enthusiasm was tremendous. Most of the crew thought that Dakar would fall without resistance. And for these Norwegians, stale and jaded after months of captivity, this spelt freedom at last. Excitement grew when a motor-launch with white flag and tricolour appeared out of the mist moving towards the inner quays. Though the haze blanketed the off-shore Allied armada from sight, it was immediately assumed that the launch carried envoys from de Gaulle coming to arrange a peaceful take-over of the town. The minutes dragged by as the men on the *Lidvard* waited tensely. Then the unexpectedly quick return of the launch told them its own story: that de Gaulle's approach had been rejected. This was confirmed when firing was heard, apparently from one of the shore batteries. The Norwegians realized there would be no Gaullist take-over without fighting.

There was failure, too, in another direction. Boislambert, in his efforts to rally support within the town, had met frustration everywhere. His nocturnal sabotage work had taken him longer than expected, and he still had much to do. Around dawn he visited the colonel commanding coast artillery, known to him as a Gaullist partisan, to warn him of de Gaulle's imminent arrival and urge him to order his batteries not to open fire. To his dismay the elderly colonel told him that he had just been relieved of his command and could do nothing. With time pressing, he made other calls; but all his likely supporters now had reasons for crying off. Finally he made his way to the docks, to establish contact, as previously planned, with d'Argenlieu's party. He arrived there in time to see the launches moving off after the arrest threat. According to one account, he had just reached the end of the quay when he spotted a squad of soldiers with automatic weapons poised to fire on the retreating boats. He called out angrily and managed to stop them. But this action drew on him the suspicious looks of the sailors and, with his Gaullist companion Bissagnet, who had now joined him, he hurried away into the town.

Throughout the Allied convoy the day had started early. In warships and transports, crews and personnel were at their action stations before 5 am. The atmosphere was not always grim and serious. In the destroyer *Dragon* it suggested 'a prologue to a peace-time picnic party.' No one on board, noted one of her officers, seemed to be worrying that soon they might be engaged in battle, killing or being killed. 'We eat our breakfasts, throwing most of the eggs over the side because they are bad. We drink water out of gin bottles. The telephone system crackles with weak jokes passing from one part of the ship to another.'[3] The sense of unreality was increased by the heavy mist, through which the ships appeared to each other as no more than dim shapes. In the words of an officer on the transport *Ettrick*, it was 'as thick as in London but white and stagnant.'[4] At 6 am visibility from the cruiser *Cumberland* was described as 'very hazy'—a state of things that left the captain none too sanguine about the coming operation, for thus early he forecast 'a little "Sticky" developing with "Happy" (meaning Menace would run into some trouble).' Forty minutes later, when the envoys' launches were reported heading for the harbour, he was no more confident, predicting that d'Argenlieu would 'very soon be on his way out again.'[5] If hopes were higher elsewhere in the convoy, the clinging murk and the lack of hard news as to how the first moves were going was inducing a general uncertainty, an uncomfortable sense of waiting.

Long before dawn, on the bridge of the *Westernland*, de Gaulle and Spears had been standing anxiously peering into the fog. Dismayed by this confounding of all their expectations, they were counting on it being dispelled by the rising sun. The ship had been aroused by a bugle call at 4 am. After a snatched breakfast, troops attached to the Spears Mission stood by in steel helmets and bulky lifebelts, in readiness for immediate action. Detailed orders had been prepared for the Mission, for 'D I Day and in the Event of Landing.'[6] There were directions for 'Dress and Equipment' specifying inter alia that 'in order to avoid risk or blistering or burning, shirt sleeves will be turned down and either slacks or long shorts, turned down and tucked inside hose tops or puttees, will be worn, with ankle boots. Those in possession of gloves will wear them . . .' Under 'Action Stations' all officers and other ranks not detailed for special duties were to parade on the starboard promenade deck at 0500 hours and remain there until further orders. Officers ordered for special duties numbered 19; and—such was de Gaulle's expectation of making the shore that first day—many of them had precise instructions what to do 'on landing.'

At 5.30 am a bugle blew for 'zero hour.' Soon after, the two Lucioles passed overhead, followed by the leaflet-dropping Swordfish. At the muffled sound of anti-aircraft fire coming from the shore, the Free French on board looked apprehensive. To de Gaulle and Spears the gunfire, along with the signalled news of the Ouakam reverse, boded ill for the reception of the envoys. Reports came of British aircraft being shot down in the sea and, with them, orders that on grounds of safety no ship was to stop to pick up survivors. As the light strengthened, de Gaulle had a signaller stand by him on the bridge, though it was doubtful what use he would be in the steadily closing visibility.

Shortly before 8 am de Gaulle learnt of the *Savorgnan de Brazza* being fired at as it stood off Dakar harbour awaiting the envoys' launches. His response was decisive. He strode to the wireless cabin to launch another radio *démarche* at Dakar. His message went out at 8.07: '. . . I am persuaded that I shall have to help the garrison and population. If this happens the operation will be confined to Frenchmen. But the *Savorgnan de Brazza* has just been fired on. If such opposition continues, enormous Allied forces which are backing me would come into action, with very serious consequences. I do not wish to contemplate this. I am sure that good sense and reason will prevail and that everything will go off without any regrettable incidents. I await the answer . . .'[7]

As de Gaulle was speaking, other Free Frenchmen were heading in to Dakar harbour. Detachments in the sloops *Commandant Dominé* and *Commandant Duboc* were about to land as a follow-up force to the envoys. They had got thus far because they had been mistaken in the fog for Dakar-based vessels. But the commander of the *Richelieu*, to whom their approach was reported, became suspicious when he failed to identify them, and telephoned Admiral Landriau. On Landriau's orders the *Richelieu* stopped them with warning shots, whereupon both sloops turned about and retired at speed to join the *Savorgnan*, which was now in open water making for the *Westernland*. At 8.50 de Gaulle was informed of this setback, and now apparently learnt for the first time of the other failures. Once more he went to the microphone to beam another stern warning to Dakar. 'Lone figure in khaki drill at wireless set,' noted Captain Mitchell. 'Doorway crammed with eager listeners.'[8]

'The authorities at Dakar,' intoned de Gaulle, 'have refused to receive the officers I had sent them. Fire has been opened on the three sloops by the *Richelieu* and the batteries of Gorée Island. If my ships and my French troops cannot fulfil their mission, the overwhelming Allied forces which are with me will take the matter in their hands. Come, good Frenchmen of Dakar, there is still time. Impose your will on those responsible, who are firing on Frenchmen!'[9]

It was a question how many people in Dakar heard these warnings from across the fog-bound water. In any case, as regards help from the local population, time had already run out. As if in confirmation, 30 minutes later de Gaulle received this signal from the wounded d'Argenlieu, who had been picked up by the *Savorgnan*: 'We are confronted by an organized and determined resistance. No sympathetic response apparent among the population.'[10] And before 10 am d'Argenlieu was aboard the *Westernland*, reporting to de Gaulle personally. In a bleak review, he related all that had happened since the Ouakam landing.

Aboard the *Westernland* the atmosphere was now tense. The men had been up since well before dawn, keyed-up for action, and hours later they were still waiting, while the news—what there was of it—grew steadily more discouraging. There was anxious speculation about the next move. 'Was it to be a bombardment?' queried Mitchell. 'Shall we have to smash them up?' What was certain was that, in the first hours of Operation Menace, everything had gone wrong. The attempt to take Ouakam airfield had failed, d'Argenlieu's mission to the Governor-General and service chiefs had been ignominiously rebuffed, and there were no signs of support for him within Dakar itself. And, perhaps the unkindest cut of all, the intimidating Allied armada that was standing off Dakar to help persuade the authorities to accept a Free French landing was blanketed from sight by a fog that no one had foretold.

The Dakar authorities had reacted quickly to the emergency. Thirty minutes after the tract-dropping raid, the general alarm was sounded and reservists ordered out. Admiral Landriau moved into his underground command post at the harbour, where he was linked with the main defence command post and had visual contact with the *Richelieu*. He directed Admiral Bourrague, who had just landed from the cruiser *Georges Leygues*, to maintain liaison with the Governor-General and the Commander-in-Chief, General Barrau. At the same time Bourrague's Chief-of-Staff, Captain Rebuffel, reported to the Defence Commander, General Picart. The landing at Ouakam and the arrival of the envoys, of which Landriau was informed soon after, convinced him that an attack was imminent. He warned the defence command post and Admiral Lacroix, who took station on the *Richelieu*.

Shortly before eight the Governor-General, Pierre Boisson,

called a meeting of service chiefs and senior government officials in his office and formally declared a state of siege, putting Dakar under the military control of General Barrau. On the vital matter of internal security, it was decided to arrest leading Gaullist sympathizers. Barrau swiftly gave orders for the round-up of suspects, and by 8.30 the police had gone into action.

Their catch was not large—a mere fifteen, including prominent citizens like the Mayor of Dakar and the President of the Chamber of Commerce. In addition there was a handful of agitators caught trying to foment some sort of demonstration. To prevent trouble, truck-loads of troops patrolled the streets, but they had little to do. For in these first hours of the great day when de Gaulle had come to liberate the city, the hoped-for crowds of welcoming supporters were just not there. Stories would be told of massed Free French partisans surging through the streets (allegedly stirred up by Boislambert's companion Bissagnet, who had been operating in the native Medina quarter earlier that day), and of a delegation calling on Boisson to accept the entry of de Gaulle.[11] But there is no real evidence for this. The hard truth was that whatever popular support for de Gaulle had simmered underground in the past months, it now, at the testing moment, failed to emerge. Almost certainly, it had never been an important factor. And even if it had now erupted into action, it would have been quickly suppressed by Barrau's troops and the police.

Meanwhile Landriau warned the Toulon squadron to raise steam, and disperse into the outer roads, and ordered the submarines *Persée* and *Ajax* to patrol specific areas of the coast and sea approaches. The coast gunners in their string of forts, the garrison troops in their strong-points around the harbour, the flyers and ground crews out at Ouakam airfield, had all completed their preparations, and now they waited. What they were waiting for, no one precisely knew, for the fog made it impossible to see much beyond the harbour. The Allied armada, somewhere away off-shore, was invisible—an unknown quantity. Then came a lucky sighting. The Dakar sloop *Calais*, on routine patrol some six miles south of Cap Manuel, almost ran

into the convoy. She headed back to harbour to report the presence of two battleships, three cruisers, some destroyers and a
dozen transports. Landriau flashed the news to the defence
command post with the warning that this formidable assem-
blage indicated a landing at any moment.

But in the shrouding fog, Landriau could only guess at the
'enemy's' intentions. And if uncertainty prevailed on shore, it
was worse among the Allied armada. On every vessel, from
Cunningham's flagship to the smallest auxiliary, there was the
same puzzled query: what was happening? Aboard the *Barham*,
where all the military staff were assembled on the admiral's
bridge, peering shorewards, there was considerable annoyance
that de Gaulle had 'jumped the gun.' He had made his opening
broadcast some 44 minutes before the agreed time, hardly giving
the leaflet raid the chance to take effect. His emissaries and the
follow-up troops had also gone in too early, again nullifying the
impact of the leaflets. (It was found later that by the time the
envoys landed, all civilians had been confined to their homes
and the leaflets were lying unread about the streets. And it was
to be asked whether de Gaulle's premature broadcast had
helped the defences by giving them an early alert.)

For some ships the only signs that anything was going on at
all were the occasional sounds of aircraft somewhere in the
murk or of muffled gunfire from the shore. The garbled and
contradictory signals passing between the ships increased the
confusion. Lack of information bred weird rumours. On the
Cumberland, for instance, the reported approach of a French
flying-boat led to the suggestion that Dakar's Governor-
General and Naval Commander-in-Chief were aboard.[12] Worst
of all, the inaction and the ominous quiet were beginning to
affect morale. 'It was becoming difficult to suppress the feeling
that impetus was being lost,' noted Spears on the *Westernland*,
'that the fog, like a slimy jelly-fish, was gradually enfolding us,
depriving us of movement.'[13] The one plain fact, increasingly
obvious as time dragged on, was that the operation was not
going according to plan. And soon there was sudden violent
confirmation of this. Shortly after 10 am, in a momentary

clearance of the fog, the big guns of Cap Manuel opened up, to land a salvo of shells around the *Barham* and a destroyer ahead of her.

CHAPTER X

MENACE DAY ONE (cont.) — FIASCO AT RUFISQUE

Cunningham had unwittingly made himself a target when he had led his force to within less than two miles of Dakar shortly before, in support of de Gaulle's sloops. If his aim was to show himself and thereby persuade the Dakar authorities into accepting a Free French landing, then his action marked the second setback to Operation Menace. De Gaulle's own men had been brusquely rebuffed, and now it was clear that Dakar was not going to be scared by the presence of supporting British warships. And to prove that this opening salvo was not just a token demonstration, the shore batteries continued to fire. Despite the muffling fog the shooting was described as 'extremely accurate,' though no hits were registered. The British ships, circling slowly in the murk, did not reply. But around 10.15, Cunningham, growing increasingly angry, signalled the shore: 'If you continue to fire on my ships, I shall be forced to reply.' From General Barrau came the curt response: 'Retire to a distance of 20 miles or fire will go on.'[1]

On the *Westernland*, de Gaulle was feeling bitterly frustrated. All his opening moves had gone wrong, and now Dakar had opened fire. But he was still stubbornly refusing to accept defeat. At 10.30 he suggested to Cunningham that the British should fire a few rounds at the *Richelieu* and the Gorée batteries, after which the French sloops should make another attempt to enter harbour. If this failed, he urged that Plan Charles—the Free

French landing at nearby Rufisque—should be tried. Cunningham sent no immediate reply; and now, at 11 o'clock, de Gaulle sent a peremptory call to Boisson: 'I demand that the Dakar authorities inform me that they are no longer opposing the landing of troops under my orders. At all events my forces, like those of the British, will reply to those firing on them.'[2]

Before Boisson had time to answer, de Gaulle's threat had materialized. A rain of British shells was crashing around the harbour area. Cunningham's patience had finally run out. Enraged at the continuing fire on his ships, around 11 o'clock he ordered them to reply. Now it was open battle—the thing that the Menace commanders had wanted above all to avoid. No doubt this was equally unwelcome to Boisson. But the only effect of the British action was to harden his fighting mood still further. Back went his retort to de Gaulle: 'Confirm to you that we shall oppose by force any landing. You have taken the responsibility for shedding French blood. Let that responsibility remain yours. Blood has already flowed.'[3]

Amid the shifting fog, 15-inch salvoes from the *Barham* and *Resolution* pounded into their targets in a half-hour-long duel with the guns of the *Richelieu*, the Vichy cruisers and the Cap Manuel and Gorée forts. Damage and casualties were caused on both sides. For the British the worst blow was a direct hit on the *Cumberland* that holed her engine-room, killing several ratings and forcing her to retire. Two destroyers were also damaged. In Dakar harbour the *Richelieu* was straddled, and shells fell in the town's crowded native quarter, demolishing houses and a hospital. Some of the population panicked, and long lines of fleeing Africans herded out along the Dakar–Rufisque road on foot, on bicycles, and any kind of transport they could muster.

Out in the open roads off Gorée Island, the French submarine *Persée* sank after being hit and set on fire by the *Dragon*. 'Clouds of water as the salvo brackets the submarine,' an officer of the *Dragon* noted. 'A bright flash close to the conning-tower shows that a shell has found the target. Through binoculars it is possible to see men pouring out of her conning-tower. Some jump into the sea. The submarine is down by the head, listing heavily to starboard.' On the *Barham*'s orders, the *Dragon* closed the stricken *Persée* to pick up survivors. This meant running right in under Gorée Island, whose buildings and concrete gun emplacements loomed clearly through the mist. 'Ahead of us lie the anti-submarine boom and the boom defence vessels,' wrote the officer. 'Beyond are the masts and funnels of the shipping in the harbour. There too is the grim silhouette of the *Richelieu*.'⁴ But the *Dragon* was not to stay in action long. Soon after, she was straddled by a rain of shells and showered with splinters from near misses. Holed in 48 places and with men wounded, she was withdrawn and allocated the role of convoy escort. Henceforth she was to follow the battle very much at second-hand.

Right in the line of fire were the merchant ships, moored beyond the inner harbour. Salvoes from the British warships plummeted among them, bringing death and destruction. The liner *Porthos* was hit, and eight crew members killed. The Danish motor ship *Tacoma* was struck amidships and set on fire. The flames spread to the nearby Swedish ship *Korsholm*, and as the *Tacoma* was being towed away the hawser broke, leaving the burning vessel right in the middle of the anchored ships. Drifting like a 'huge pyre', she narrowly avoided the *Lidvard*—herself shaken by a near miss, with shell splinters all over the deck. Some crews who had earlier gone ashore hurried back among bursting shells. A Jugoslav skipper barely escaped death when a shell landed near him, killing 17 men. For these merchant crews who had welcomed the approach of de Gaulle's envoys so hopefully a few hours before, this was a shattering experience.

After some thirty minutes the firing stopped and the British force hauled off. For Cunningham it can hardly have been a more unsatisfactory action. Visibility was atrocious, communications lamentable, and the engagement itself purposeless except from the retaliatory point of view. Certainly it was not likely to change the defenders' minds about accepting de Gaulle. All in all, at this moment the prospects for Menace's quick success looked black. The mid-morning situation, as seen from the *Barham*, was recorded as follows: 'Opposition to de Gaulle 100 per cent from the authorities, substantial from the French Navy and partial from some of the batteries. Civilian population unable or unwilling to support. Opposition to British forces wholehearted from authorities, forts and probably French Navy. French Air Force adopting a passive attitude towards both Free French and British. Attitude of French troops unknown, but possibly General de Gaulle's agents in Dakar might have had some success with army as these appeared to have had with the Air Force.'[5]

On the transports, slowly circling far from the shore, personnel had been almost literally in the dark as to what was going on. 'All this time,' noted Spears, 'we [on the *Westernland*] only occasionally got a glimpse of British destroyers, and once of battleships. *Pennland* and food ship *Belgravia* were only ones visible, following us closely. Occasionally very heavy firing was heard, and from this time on situation was extremely obscure, visual signalling was only occasionally possible, the wireless phone never could be used for conversation and the W/T was well overworked so that there was great delay in getting off and receiving messages.'[6] He added later: 'As we stood on the drenched bridge, helpless, blind and uninformed, hope of success otherwise than by a landing which would take Dakar from the rear, fell away minute by minute.'[7]

Plan Charles: this now seemed the only move that could rescue Operation Menace from failure. De Gaulle had already suggested to the British commanders that the plan should be tried as soon as it was clear that the direct approach to Dakar had failed. But on the *Barham* Cunningham and Irwin were wrestling with a situation that was becoming more obscure and confused every minute. Starved of proper information owing to the fog and near-breakdown of communications, they could come to no firm decision. So hazy were they about the situation that at 12.15 they signalled de Gaulle on the *Westernland* requesting immediate information on his intentions. 'We on the other hand,' noted Spears, 'were waiting to be told whether the situation was ripe for Charles.' After hurried consultation, de Gaulle replied at 12.50 that he was in favour of Plan Charles. Apparently the *Barham* never received his signal; and 50 minutes later de Gaulle had to repeat the message. But already eight minutes before this the British commanders had signalled their decision to de Gaulle. Charles would go ahead at 3.30 that afternoon. 'Situation then again became extremely obscure owing to difficulty of communication,' was Spears' summing-up.[8]

But even now de Gaulle had not abandoned hopes of avoiding further violence. Making one more effort at peaceful persuasion, at 3 pm, he launched his most impassioned broadcast appeal to the defenders: 'Frenchmen of Dakar, one of your fellow-countrymen, a French officer, is speaking to you. Are you going to let this tragic misunderstanding continue? We are bringing you liberty, and at the same time provisions, and arms for your defence. We come to you as brothers, with open arms . . . Frenchmen, there is still time. Do not hesitate a minute longer. We can free you from the unworthy leaders who are driving you straight to ruin and dishonour. It rests with you to take the path of honour and victory. Let your hearts be high. Rally yourselves to the forces of General de Gaulle!'[9]

To this there was no reply. And now, with Dakar implacably closed to him and any direct approach to it from the sea ruled out, only the Rufisque operation remained. Tactically a Free French landing here might well be possible but, seeing the intractable mood of Dakar's defenders and their undoubted military capability, could it really avail to get de Gaulle into Dakar itself?

The question never had to be answered, for Plan Charles was to prove as big a fiasco for the Allies as that of the morning.

At a final meeting on the *Westernland* it was decided that the landing should be carried out in two waves. The first would be of *fusiliers marins* from the three sloops *Savorgnan*, *Commandant Duboc* and *Commandant Dominé*, along with the vessel *President Houduce*, and the second of brigade troops who would be waiting on the *Westernland* and *Pennland* at a point six miles south-west of Rufisque. It was thought that the defences at Rufisque—a two-gun battery of 95's with a small contingent of native troops —could easily be neutralized. Meanwhile, to prevent interference by the Vichy cruisers, Cunningham's force would be mounting guard over the exits from Dakar harbour.

Soon after 2 o'clock the sloops moved off towards Rufisque. Behind them were the transports, making for their own rendezvous. But at 3.30 this Free French flotilla was spotted by a reconnaissance plane from Ouakam, together with some ten British destroyers ('une dizaine') making towards Dakar harbour.[10] Admiral Lacroix ordered out the destroyer *Audacieux* to investigate. Hardly had the *Audacieux* cleared the boom when, in the fog, she almost ran into a British cruiser. Before she could get into position to fire her torpedoes she received a salvo at close range. Hit in her forward magazine she immediately became a blazing inferno, with 40 men killed or missing and 100 wounded. She would continue to burn for 36 hours and eventually drift ashore near Rufisque.

The *Audacieux* had been hit and disabled at 4.30. Lacroix, now certain that something was 'on', ordered out the two Vichy cruisers, *Georges Leygues* and *Montcalm*. Evading the patrolling British force by using a hazardously shallow and little-used channel, the cruisers edged out into the broad curve of Rufisque bay and moved slowly south without making any contacts. By 5.20 they were off Rufisque itself—almost at the precise moment that the Free French sloops were heading shorewards, less than a mile away. Not far to the south-west of them were the *Westernland* and *Pennland*, now waiting at what they thought was their agreed rendezvous (in fact they were miles off it). If the French cruisers had seen them, both the sloops and the transports could have been blown out of the water. Instead, they were saved by the mist that still hung relentlessly over sea and shore. Suspecting nothing, the cruisers then turned and made for home. It was like some bizarre game of blind man's buff. If the fates had so far been cruelly against de Gaulle, now in this narrowest of shaves they were with him indeed.

But while the Vichy cruisers were unaware of the attackers' approach, the attackers knew all about the Vichy cruisers. A British plane had spotted them through the fog and was regularly reporting their movements to the convoy. For the Free French sloops, now nearing the shore at Rufisque, the situation began to look uncomfortable. And soon after 5 pm the *Commandant Dominé*, uneasily conscious that two hostile warships were lurking unseen somewhere near them, signalled the *Savorgnan*, the command sloop, asking what to do if she met the cruisers. 'If you're fired on, reply,' answered the *Savorgnan*. There was reason for the *Dominé*'s men to be worried. 'As the hour for landing approached,' noted an officer aboard the *Westernland*, 'the fog thickened until, looking down from the bridge of the leading troopship, the surface of the sea became invisible.'[11]

The *Duboc* and *Dominé* proceeded in line astern towards the shore, with the *Savorgnan* a mile behind. The latter had now stopped and was putting her boats in the water in order to disembark her landing-party. And just as the *Duboc* was approaching the port's jetty, closely followed by the *Dominé*, the 95 battery at the foot of Rufisque's lighthouse opened up at point-blank range. The guns of the *Dominé* and *Savorgnan* immediately replied. A shell tore into the *Duboc*, killing one man and wounding five. Meanwhile the *Dominé* managed to take avoiding action under a smoke-screen. Then the guns of the shore battery suddenly stopped, silenced by fire from the *Savorgnan*'s 5.5-inch guns at 2,500 yards. The shore battery was in fact not hit but had been abandoned by the native gunners after the battery commander had been wounded.

But the *Savorgnan* had not finished. Her commander now determined to land his boats on the beach to the south of Rufisque pier and asked the *Dominé* to cover the landing. But this attempt was equally unsuccessful. The *Dominé* was caught by withering fire from a strong-point overlooking the beach, and signalled the *Savorgnan*: 'Impossible to hold on.' The sloops returned a few rounds and then, just after 6, the *Savorgnan*'s commander called off the attack. Now, in fact, the matter was out of his hands. A few minutes before, he himself had received this signal from the *Westernland*: 'Plan Charles ended . . . Request that you rejoin *Westernland, Pennland* . . .'[12] The *Savorgnan* pulled in her boats and the three sloops headed seawards in the now failing light. On the *Duboc* were five seriously wounded men, two of whom were to die soon after. The other three were moved to the *Savorgnan*, from which they were later taken aboard the *Westernland*.

The failure of Plan Charles was total. The official Spears Mission report of the action helps fill out the picture of this brief and futile clash. 'One French sloop,' it ran, 'had got alongside jetty and landed some men without opposition. Some boats also seem to have landed on beach, natives helping to haul them up. A battery on shore at Rufisque itself opened fire causing seven casualties, including three killed, several severely wounded. French sloops, though handicapped by landing operations, returned the fire and silenced battery. A good many marines were landed and were met with a certain amount of machine-gun fire from the Senegalese troops.' Significantly, the report concludes: 'Seems no doubt that landings on a big scale could have been carried out as the sea was exceptionally calm, but this would undoubtedly have been highly dangerous in view of presence of French cruisers in immediate vicinity.'[13]

Reports differ about the attitude of the troops at Rufisque. One colourful account claims that almost the whole native garrison was pro-Gaullist. Even the local commander, a Frenchman, was allegedly a Gaullist partisan and deliberately refrained from giving orders to resist the landing—possibly banking on the fact that communications with Dakar, cut during Boislambert's sabotage efforts the night before, were still out of action. But unluckily for him they had been repaired, and another officer telephoned Dakar, receiving the order to repel the attackers. The native troops made no move to obey, on the pretence that their weapons were damaged. Thereupon this officer and one other manned a gun themselves and drove off the invading force without their firing a shot.[14] Far-fetched as was this story, seemingly it contains some truth. Major Wingate, of the Spears Mission, records that 'a year later the officer commanding the Senegalese company quite firmly maintained that the resistance put up was merely token; that he and the Senegalese had no intention of continuing it, and were stunned with surprise when the Marines withdrew.'[15]

Despite the Spears Mission report, the British liaison officers aboard the three sloops all insisted that the Free French never landed at all. A British official report states: 'It is quite certain from the liaison officers' accounts that no landing took place, nor does it appear that the French transports ever approached closer than about seven miles from Rufisque. What can be stated without doubt is that Rufisque had prepared for an attempted landing . . . The (Free) French troops had not been prepared for landings against such opposition.'[16]

Lt Allen, liaison officer on the *Duboc*, noted that after the action the French officers aboard seemed indignant that no British warships had supported them. They felt too that they had been deserted by the French transports. To Allen, these Frenchmen appeared highly reluctant to fight against their compatriots. They were loud enough in their threats against the Vichy Government, but not so keen to carry out the threats. He did, however, speak highly of their courage. Lt-Commander Battine, aboard the *Savorgnan*, also remarked on the Free Frenchmen's unwillingness to fire on fellow-countrymen, even in self-defence. Admiral Muselier had apparently told them they would not have to engage the naval force at Dakar; and, assuming that they themselves would not be fired on, they were astonished at their hostile reception on this first day of Menace.[17]

But it was to the credit of those Marines that they even attempted a landing. They had had no training in using boats. And the arrangements for manning and operating these boats had been extremely casual. As Captain Mitchell relates: 'The Dutch captain [aboard the *Westernland*] asked for volunteers, 25 from the English crew—Liverpool dockside boys—25 from the Dutch crew, to man the ships' boats. Forty English volunteered including the bellhop, but only 18 Dutch. The captain congratulated the English and reviled the Dutch.'[18] Spears sums it up by saying: 'The Free French *fusiliers marins* had neither leadership nor training, not even the minimum required for brave men to dash for an objective. This led to their failure, not lack of courage.'[19]

On the *Westernland* herself the afternoon had been a succession of alarms, alerts and mishaps. First, in the fog she had approached much closer to Rufisque than was planned, moving into dangerous shallows within earshot of the shore breakers. Then two Glenn Martin planes from Dakar loomed out of the murk and passed over her at 2,000 feet. Fears ran through the ship that this might portend a bombing attack. And misgivings grew when the destroyer escort allocated to de Gaulle's ship disappeared. On top of that had come the report that the two Vichy cruisers were at large and practically on a collision course with the transports. 'De Gaulle really upset at this,' noted Spears. 'The thought crossed my mind that he feared they might demand his surrender on pain of sinking us.'[20] The flotilla hurriedly swung about and headed out of danger. As the *Westernland* wallowed on the oily swell, her troops, mainly Foreign Legion men, stood by on the decks awaiting the moment when they—the second wave—would go in. She was still near enough to Rufisque for the shore and nearby buildings to be clearly visible in the shifting mist, and bursts of gunfire to be heard. But this was as close to action as the men on the *Westernland* and *Pennland* got. For them now came the day's crowning anti-climax: the *Barham*'s signal, 'Charles is cancelled.'

At this, records Wingate, 'the scene on the *Westernland* was indescribable. Everybody was furious and could not make out what could have happened, especially when the wounded from the sloop were transferred, and it became known that we had landed (sic) and that such resistance as there was could easily have been overcome.'[21]

Once more, in this abortive Rufisque operation, everything had gone wrong. Again the chief villain was fog; but almost equally to blame were the appalling radio communications, time and again preventing transmission of vital orders and information. As Mitchell reports, the *Westernland*, owing to the limited range of her No. 11 set, could not pass messages to the *Barham*, though the *Westernland* could receive the *Barham*. Repeatedly through the afternoon the *Barham* was asking 'Where are you? Where are you?'[22] Again, the W/T telephone fixed between Spears and his deputy Colonel Williams, on the *Barham*, never worked; and there were two-hour delays on important signals as the lines became increasingly clogged. 'This was quite awful,' commented Spears.

In these vital hours confusion and uncertainty reigned supreme. Entries in the Spears Mission report on the *Westernland* reveal a grim picture of cross-purposes and misunderstandings:

'1615. We signalled we expected to arrive at point of assembly at 1650 which was to be zero hour. Meanwhile, it seems, Admiral had little knowledge of where we were. At about this time we received a signal from Admiral stating that, as result of Plan Charles could not be known in time to proceed as arranged, he proposed to issue a one-hour ultimatum to Boisson at 1600 hours, Charles continuing meanwhile.

'1620. De Gaulle informed Commanders that as result of ultimatum he was suspending landing troops from troopships for time being but meanwhile was landing marines from sloops. A signal stating 'Cancel Charles' was marked as having been received at 1639 but this cannot have been received before following signal was sent.

'1712. Signal sent asking if ultimatum had been sent [in fact it never was] and stating that Marines were being landed from sloops and adding that we were awaiting news from sloops before deciding on landing main body . . .

'1845. Admiral again called for immediate report on position of Free French ships. Our messages re our position seem to have been badly received all day.'[23]

On the *Barham* there was equal obscurity: 'No information, despite requests for position, course and speed at 1415 and 1502, of whereabouts of French transports was received till 1545, when *Devonshire* reported sighting *Westernland* at 1437, but this did little to clarify position as transports were then on opposite courses executing a turn.'[24] Irwin was later to recall the flagship's desperate attempts to contact the *Westernland*. After ordering Charles about 11 am, he said, the *Barham* continued sending signals up to 6 pm, but got no further reply as to de Gaulle's progress or intentions. Not until then was it learnt that the Free French were said to be landing at Rufisque. But as it was getting dark and the thick haze persisted, there was nothing for it but to signal 'Cancel Charles.'[25]

Even before Plan Charles's launching, de Gaulle, depressed by the events of the morning, had been growing steadily more pessimistic about it. 'There was a curious little interlude', recorded Spears, 'when, his soul sorely puzzled, de Gaulle consulted me. He felt Charles was pretty desperate and wanted to get out of it. He had just told Cunningham he would do so—he often changes his mind like that. The only excuse [for abandoning the plan] was that Cunningham had signalled that the batteries as well as the ships were in whole-hearted opposition. I made a suggestion which he adopted, but he later came to me as I was working on his text and tore it up, saying he would do Charles. Glad he did. It was rather a Gethsemane for him.'[26]

Was Plan Charles really doomed from the start? Other factors apart, could a successful landing in strength have been achieved against the moderate opposition at Rufisque? The Spears Mission report suggests that it could, but that the attempt would have been highly risky in view of the presence nearby of the Vichy cruisers. But in fact these could be discounted, as they had left the scene some time before without sighting the Free French force. Indeed, the *Dominé*'s commander, the tough and determined Lt de la Porte de Vaux, concludes that it was the cruisers that needlessly intimidated the landing force and so defeated Plan Charles. As for the formidable backing of the British warships, whose fire could easily have silenced the Rufisque guns, this de Gaulle had decided not to call upon. De Gaulle himself wrote later that the warships were occupied elsewhere and in no position to help. Moreover, not only was a landing from the transports impossible, but a few rounds from the Vichy cruisers would have been enough to sink the whole Free French flotilla. He therefore decided to sail, haul off from Rufisque and regain the open sea.

As de Gaulle said, Cunningham's force was in no position to help. The destroyers, standing off beyond the French transports, were prevented from approaching them closer for fear of collision in the fog. The main fleet, after withdrawing from the morning's engagement, lay miles out to sea. And assistance from the *Ark Royal* was impossible, as the carrier was 20 miles west of the nearest land and if her planes had taken off on an operation they could never have regained her flight-deck in the enveloping fog.

The setback at Rufisque had hit de Gaulle and Spears hard. That evening Mitchell, visiting Spears on the *Westernland*'s bridge to receive orders for the following day, found the two men wrapped in silent gloom. 'Two lone figures were seated on chairs staring blankly ahead in the direction of fast receding Dakar,' he noted. 'They were not talking or looking at each other. I saluted General Spears. There was no response. He seemed to be thinner in the face. Perspiration was streaming down his cheeks. I touched his shoulder. "Shall I dismiss the men, sir?" I asked. "What men?" came the irritable reply in a whispered voice. "Pardon me, sir, I thought I was addressing General Spears." A weary head turned to me. "I *am* General Spears," he replied. The other statue-like figure made neither sound nor movement but continued to gaze stonily ahead into the all-enveloping darkness. It was General de Gaulle.'

In London the War Cabinet received the news of the launching of Menace from Winston Churchill at five that afternoon. The Ministers were meeting, as they had for days past, in an atmosphere tense with the threat of imminent invasion. Hitler's assault barges were still massed across the Channel, and London continued to be heavily bombed; and despite one report that the latest date for invasion would be the 21st September, there was no certainty yet that the danger was over. Now, amid their pressing cares and anxieties, Ministers would have welcomed some hopeful news about Menace—the operation that had so far been so ill-starred. But the tidings that Churchill gave them were not encouraging: at first the situation had seemed favourable despite the presence of thick fog, but a further message had indicated opposition by Dakar, an engagement had taken place between the British warships and the shore batteries, after which the warships had withdrawn into the fog, and in the afternoon de Gaulle was attempting a landing at nearby Rufisque, under cover of fog. 'Rather gloomy,' recorded Sir Arthur Cadogan, who was present.[28]

More details of the day's reverses which reached Churchill during the evening only hardened the resolve of this stubborn and determined fighter not to abandon the enterprise now. Soon after 10 o'clock, without consulting his Cabinet colleagues, he signalled Cunningham: 'Having begun, we must go on to the end. Stop at nothing.'[29]

That same afternoon the news of Menace reached Vichy to provoke anger, alarm and a series of emergency cabinet meetings. Baudouin was in conference with the Chinese Ambassador when he learnt of it through a telephone call from Darlan. Pierre Laval, Deputy Prime Minister, was then informed, and at 4 o'clock a meeting was held, presided over by Marshal Pétain and attended by Laval, Baudouin, Darlan, Generals Huntziger and Bergereau and Admiral Platon. 'We were very upset by this news,' noted Baudouin, especially at the fact that a Frenchman (de Gaulle) had been so 'short-sighted' as to put his country—in the event of Dakar falling—into the dangerous position of risking a German invasion of North Africa. As Baudouin saw it, the whole structure of the armistice would thereby collapse. It was decided to send at once to Dakar a force of planes from Morocco, and Darlan's proposal for a reprisal air attack on Gibraltar, to be mounted next day by planes from Algiers was unanimously approved. One thing on which the assembled Ministers were implacably resolved was that Boisson must continue to resist at all costs. Baudouin drafted an order to him to this effect, which Pétain approved and signed for immediate transmission to Dakar.[30]

The message went out, to be read that evening by Dakar's embattled Governor-General: 'France follows with emotion and confidence your resistance to the treason of partisans and to the British aggression. Under your high authority, Dakar gives an example of courage and loyalty. The whole nation is proud of your attitude and of the determination of the forces you command. I congratulate you and express to you all my confidence. Philippe Pétain.'[31]

This heartening tribute was matched by a message that Boisson himself had broadcast to the people of Dakar at seven o'clock: 'The British fleet opened fire at Dakar! No military objective was hit. The native hospital was struck, and women and children have been wounded. Dakar has answered the call to revolt by the most absolute calm. Dakar will not submit . . . There is no glory to be found here, but only French blood to shed.'[32]

After a further Cabinet meeting at 5 pm, Baudouin summoned members of the French and foreign press to inform them of the Allied assault. At 10.15 Pétain sent for him. Baudouin found the old Marshal deeply upset by the events at Dakar, and urged on him that France must take advantage of them to obtain from Germany a firm undertaking that West Africa, now being stoutly defended by the Germans themselves, should never have to accept German or Italian occupation. As to all the British and Free French propaganda about the presence of Germans in Dakar, Pétain agreed with Baudouin that this was false.

Baudouin was particularly incensed at the British attitude over the affair. That day, in his diary, he lamented that all his warnings to Britain about rash actions that might provoke intervention by Germany, had gone for nothing. Three days before, he noted, Sir Samuel Hoare had reassured the Vichy Ambassador in Madrid about Britain's pacific intentions *vis-à-vis* France's colonies. 'Why this duplicity?' added the aggrieved Foreign Minister.[33]

While the guns clashed at distant Dakar, at home each side

quickly brought its propaganda weapon into play. In London that night the Ministry of Information issued a statement for publication in next day's papers. 'Recent reports,' it said, 'have shown that the Germans were making persistent efforts to bring Dakar under their control, and the movement of French ships from Toulon to Dakar, which clearly would not have been effected without German permission, gave further evidence of the attempt that was in contemplation. In view of the fact that a considerable element of the population were opposed to the Vichy Government's policy of subservience to Berlin and had declared in favour of Free France, General de Gaulle decided to proceed with a Free French Force to Dakar to assist those elements which supported his cause. He arrived at Dakar this morning and summoned his followers to rally to the flag of Free France. Resistance seems to have been encountered, but the situation is not yet fully clear. General de Gaulle's Free French Force is accompanied by a British force which will lend him full support.'[34]

In Vichy, at the instigation of Baudouin himself, the Agence Havas put out a statement proclaiming: '. . . This criminal act has been preceded by certain signs. Two days ago, in fact, a French supply convoy encountered British units in the Atlantic which ordered it to turn back. The French ships did not fire. Today it is the English who opened fire . . . The English action surpasses in gravity their attack on the French ships at Mers-el-Kebir, where they were able to invoke some sort of pre-text and claim that in theory the French ships could join the Italian and German fleets. This evil pretext can no longer be advanced. The English had no reason to fear any threat from Dakar, where there were only French forces. Thus it is through pure greed for colonies and the desire to destroy the French Empire that Great Britain has committed this fresh act.'[35]

It mattered not that Britain had no designs on the French Empire, or that there was no German move afoot to gain control of Dakar: as ammunition to boost the causes of the French and British, the charges had a specious ring of truth. The irony of the situation was that, in the matter of Dakar,

Britain and Vichy France had one thing in common far more important than their differences: both were determined to keep the Germans out of it.

In the gathering darkness de Gaulle's flotilla had headed away from Rufisque to a point well south of Dakar. On the *Westernland* there was anxious speculation as to what would happen now. The general view was that as the Free French effort had failed the next move was up to the British. This meant the bombardment of Dakar and a possible British landing. De Gaulle had no idea what the British commanders intended, but he had to find out. And late that evening he signalled the *Barham* asking for their appreciation of the situation. Cunningham and Irwin were in an unenviable position. Throughout the day they had watched de Gaulle's effort founder in near disaster, and Cunningham had been forced to intervene himself. Now they had the hard task of deciding whether to call off the operation—with all the humiliation which that entailed—or assume the repugnant job of shelling Dakar into submission and thereafter landing British troops. In the event they were saved a decision. It was made for them, at the highest level. Around 11 o'clock Cunningham received Churchill's terse uncompromising order: 'Having begun, we must go on to the end. Stop at nothing.'

Thus covered, they replied forthwith to de Gaulle that they were assuming the situation was 'Nasty'—calling for a full-scale assault—and that they were framing their plans accordingly. De Gaulle was asked also whether he agreed with the issue of an ultimatum to Dakar's Governor-General, which Cunningham was proposing to make. By this, Boisson was to be told that if he did not accede by 6 am next day to the Allied demand to admit the Free French to Dakar, the British would proceed with a bombardment, later landing troops if necessary. For good measure, the signal ended by quoting Churchill's fighting directive. Studying the commanders' message, de Gaulle had one reservation: on no account must his forces be thought to be involved in the projected action. He replied agreeing that the situation was 'Nasty', and stressing that it should be made clear in the ultimatum that the operation was purely British and that the Free French had been withdrawn.

For everyone concerned with Menace it had been a day of fiasco and frustration. If all had gone well, de Gaulle would have been installed in Dakar by mid-morning, hailed by welcoming crowds and accepted—if with less enthusiasm—by the civil and military authorities. Instead, he had been ignominiously repulsed, with shooting and bloodshed on both sides. And now it looked as if Dakar would have to be bombarded into submission. So much for de Gaulle's high hopes of a few weeks before. In his cabin that night Spears wearily confided to his diary: 'Worn out. It is a failure, serious in every way; also for me, who pressed for the plan.' It says something for his and de Gaulle's resilience that at this dark moment he was able to add: 'But I am not discouraged or down—de Gaulle's moral is good.'

CHAPTER XI

MENACE DAY TWO—
FAILURE CONFIRMED

The ultimatum that Cunningham had proposed went out from the *Barham* at 1.30 am on the 24th. Though issued in the name of the Joint Commanders, it was really the work of de Gaulle, who had approved its terms and largely composed it himself. If de Gaulle's previous calls had failed to move the Dakar authorities, this blunt and peremptory demand, with its harping once more on Dakar's 'pro-German' stance, was virtually guaranteed to be rejected out of hand. It ran as follows:

'To the Governor and People of Dakar. General de Gaulle informs you—and us, the commanders of the British naval and military forces—that you have prevented him from landing his forces and re-supplying Dakar; and that later your forts and troops opened fire on our ships, though without result. Your attitude causes us to believe that Dakar may at any moment be handed over by you to the common enemy. Because of the importance of this base in relation to the war, and because its occupation by the enemy would mean the oppression of its inhabitants, the Allies deem it their duty to take all necessary steps to prevent its seizure. General de Gaulle has no wish that Frenchmen should fight other Frenchmen, and has therefore withdrawn his forces; but our forces are ready . . .

'We have the honour to inform you that if, by 6 am on the 24th, you have not handed over your powers to General de Gaulle, the strong forces at our disposal will come into action.

Once the action has started, it will continue until the defences of Dakar are entirely destroyed and the town is occupied by troops who will be ready to carry out their duty. Only the announcement that our conditions are accepted can stop the execution of this step, and the troops will not land if you decide to join your compatriots for the liberation of your country and sever your attachment to the enemy who holds France at his mercy. There can be no compromise. Announce your acceptance before 6 o'clock and avoid bloodshed.'[1]

On receiving the ultimatum Boisson summoned to the Defence Command Post an urgent meeting of senior colleagues: General Barrau, Admiral Landriau, General Gama and Inspector-General Boulmer. In the stuffy heat of the command post they studied the *démarche*. 'What shall we say?' asked Boisson, grasping a note-pad and pencil. Everyone seems to have decided on the response from the start. There was no question of acceding to the British demand, and the matter of not defending to the last was not even discussed. Somebody suggested a single, forceful monosyllabic word—vulgar but of unmistakable significance. But it was recalled that the word had just been used in similar circumstances by a naval commander in the French Pacific possession of Noumea. Finally Boisson, seated on a mattress and drinking from a bottle of tepid lemonade, scribbled the brief uncompromising answer: 'France has entrusted Dakar to me. I shall defend it to the end.' Landriau hurried to the nearest telephone to order the *Richelieu* to transmit the message to Cunningham. The time was 4.24 am.[2]

Now, however repugnant to Cunningham and the men he commanded, the British assault would have to go ahead. Their brief was plain and unequivocal: 'Stop at nothing.' But at least on this second day of Menace there was one factor that promised to ease the task of the naval gunners. The fog that had bedevilled the first day's operations had thinned, leaving only a light surface haze. With any luck this would soon dissipate under the hot African sun.

Around dawn, as Dakar's defences stood by to resist the coming onslaught, the Skuas and Swordfish of the carrier *Ark Royal* prepared for take-off against Dakar harbour; their targets, the *Richelieu*, the Vichy cruisers and the forts. And Cunningham's heavy ships moved in from their night positions to assume their bombardment stations. But with the low-lying mist still hampering visibility, the warships had to edge in closer to shorten their range. Meanwhile the attack was being opened with a successful strike against a second Vichy submarine.

At 7 am the *Ajax*, on patrol some eight miles south-west of Gorée Island, found herself in full view of the *Barham* and *Resolution*. She immediately dived, and despite the ominous ping of the Asdic soundings that told him he was being hunted, her commander decided to surface for an attack. But a hit on his periscope was followed by a rain of depth-charges that sent the *Ajax* to the bottom, badly damaged. After some 90 minutes, with the water-level mounting dangerously, she was forced to the surface. Her commander gave the order to scuttle. As the *Ajax* slowly sank, a party from the destroyer *Fortune*, which was standing nearby, boarded her and took off her crew.

Mr B. G. Gallaway, a member of the *Fortune*'s boarding-party, remembers the episode. 'I was ordered to join as interpreter. It was a chance to speak again in the language I had learnt in a French monastery before the war.' Later, he says, 'the French crew came aboard and I was told to chat with them. I discovered that the crew was split into two camps—pro- and anti-Vichy. The pro-Vichy told me nothing . . . I was shocked to hear expressed the genuinely felt opinion that Dunkirk was not a glorious recovery from utter disaster but that in the eyes of many Frenchmen the British had acted cowardly in jumping into the boats and leaving France.' This, from anti-Vichy Frenchmen, suggests how bitter may have been the feeling among Dakar's pro-Vichy sailors.

Gallaway has other memories, too, of this eposode. 'After the crew had been taken off,' he recalls, 'we examined the interior [of the *Ajax*] and passed a case containing a new pair of binoculars. The *Fortune* at the time was short of this article of equipment, so I took it with me onto the upper deck. The Boarding-Officer informed me that I could not remove this, even though the ship was going down, because that would constitute looting. To me, at the time, that was an overstrict interpretation of the rules . . .' But Gallaway's clearest recollection of the day is of the battleships *Resolution* and *Barham*, with their attendant destroyers, 'all flying their battle ensigns. The spouts of water rising from the shore batteries' shells were of different colours for sighting purposes . . . This was an occasion on which I would very much have liked to be an oil painter.'[3]

Just as the *Ajax* was running into trouble, six Skuas from the *Ark Royal* zoomed over Dakar harbour to bomb the *Richelieu*. In the surface haze the best they could achieve was a near miss. Soon after, six Swordfish attacked the Cap Manuel battery but did little damage. Then at 9 o'clock, with the *Richelieu* again the target, three out of six attacking Swordfish were shot down by ground fire and another by a fighter from Ouakam. Before this plane sank, a French vessel managed to retrieve its signal codes; and this, with the score of four British planes down, served as an early boost to the defenders' morale. But minutes later, in lengthening visibility, the British cruisers' guns roared out. And almost as their first salvo hit the harbour the *Georges Leygues* opened up.

For 30 minutes a violent artillery battle raged, at a range of 14,000 yards. Salvoes from the *Barham*, *Resolution*, *Australia* and *Devonshire* pounded into the harbour area and around the forts. But despite the intensity of the fire, no French ship was hit. This was largely because the cruisers had moved out into the roadstead, where they kept up a continuous zig-zagging movement amid the 50-odd merchant ships anchored there. They were further protected by a dense smoke-screen laid across the entrance by two destroyers. Less lucky were some of the merchantmen. The *Lidvard*, clear of the smoke-screen, was once more right in the line of fire. From behind her came the salvoes of the *Georges Leygues*, roaring close overhead, and around her crashed shell after shell from the British ships, damaging several nearby vessels. 'Nerve-racking morning,' wrote one of her crew.

Soon after 10, with the harbour obscured by smoke, Cunningham called off the engagement and retired. As his force stood off to the south, three waves of Glen Martins from Ouakam launched high-level attacks on it without effect.

But Cunningham was not leaving the situation there. Whatever he personally felt about the chances of bombarding Dakar into surrender, he had his directive from Churchill. So, about 1 pm, he ordered the attack to be renewed. For some 20 minutes the broadsides from the British warships thundered onto the town, onto Gorée Island, and into the harbour and outer roads. The *Barham*, at 17,000 yards, was concentrating on the *Richelieu*; and the *Resolution*'s chief target, from 16,000 yards, was Gorée. At her mole in the harbour the *Richelieu* counted 160 shell-bursts around her but escaped with minor damage. But among the crowded merchantmen in the outer roads there was more havoc, with the *Porthos* and the oil tanker *Tacoma* hit and burning fiercely. Yet, once more, the Toulon cruisers, zig-zagging in the roads, went virtually unscathed. The defenders' main target seemed to be the *Barham*. For some 10 minutes the *Richelieu* and the Cap Manuel and Gorée batteries plastered the flagship with heavy and accurate fire. Twice she was hit, though not seriously. Throughout the brief engagement Cunningham's ships were increasingly hampered by the persistent slight haze and the dense smoke screen belching across the harbour's entrance. By 1.25 sighting had become so difficult that Cunningham ordered a cease-fire and withdrew his force southwards.

Dejectedly the commanders summed up the results of the morning's action. Neither naval nor air attacks had managed to silence any of the larger batteries—despite the two battleships' expenditure of nearly 400 15-inch rounds. The *Richelieu* was still in action and several 5.4-inch batteries had not been located. On the other hand, enemy air activity was intensifying and the defenders' will to resist seemed unimpaired. The *Ark Royal* had signalled that further prospects of successful air attack on the batteries were poor, and that reconnaissance and spotting had become increasingly hazardous. 'In these circumstances,' said the commanders' report, 'it was decided to consult de Gaulle and the force was withdrawn to a position where this could be done before dark.'[4]

Sailing untouched through the forest of shell-bursts, the men of the Vichy cruisers had during this second attack (as a historian of the battle records) felt a strange and growing confidence. As the ships crossed and recrossed the crews cheered each other wildly. By some miracle they had survived the formidable assault of Cunningham's battleships without a scratch. To these Frenchmen it was immaterial who their attackers were—British, German, Italian. They were firing on them, therefore they were 'the enemy'.

Lying off well to the south of Dakar, the men on the transports heard the distant sound of gunfire but had no idea how things were going. The only indication that they were not going well was the firing that continued through the morning. Evidently Dakar was not giving in easily. But, on the *Westernland*, de Gaulle was still hoping his appeals would be effective. Twice that morning he radioed messages to Dakar, reiterating his previous calls. He announced the Free French withdrawal from the action and the intervention of the British forces; stressed his readiness to answer the first request addressed to him to stop the fighting; attacked Dakar's leaders for their deception of the people; and ended: 'It is up to you to bring a stop to a uselessly murderous conflict. We await your call. Frenchmen of Dakar, citizens and subjects, why do you delay rallying to the Free French forces of General de Gaulle?'[5] But from Dakar, as on the previous day, there was no response.

Meanwhile, among the transports, a solemn little ceremony was taking place. The Free French were burying their dead, killed at Rufisque. Mitchell observed this from the *Westernland*: '*Savorgnan de Brazza* appeared quite close to us, flag at half-mast. Clusters of figures in tropical khaki lined up on deck, their backs to us. She gradually moved away and then a gun was fired in salute. Three Free Frenchmen, assassinated by other Frenchmen, consigned to a tropical Atlantic grave. We all stood still and saluted.'[6]

But aboard the *Ettrick*, whose troops had yet to experience action, the atmosphere was very different. The holiday mood still prevailed, the only reminder that a battle was going on being the distant rumble of the guns. 'The Goanese stewards still walked the corridors with their little gongs to announce the five-course table d'hôte,' records Lieutenant St John. 'Ivor Novello's "Dancing Years" still poured their reassuring syrup through the ship's loudspeakers.'[7]

On the *Westernland*, de Gaulle and Spears were busy drawing up an appreciation of the situation when, about 2 o'clock, Cunningham's force hove in sight from the north. Later a signal came from the *Barham* asking them to join the commanders for a conference on the flagship. Accompanied by de Gaulle's ADC, Lieutenant de Courcel, de Gaulle and Spears pitched across the choppy seas in a whaler and clambered hazardously aboard the *Barham*, to be met by Cunningham and Irwin on the admiral's bridge. With Captain Walter and Colonel Smith-Hill attending, the discussion started gloomily. As Spears relates, the atmosphere was 'rather depressing and everyone showed signs of wear and fatigue. None of the officers were shaved.'

This was the most sombre top-level meeting since the expedition had left Britain. Cunningham and Irwin were both conscious that, more than half-way through Day Two, Operation Menace had achieved nothing. Appeals, ultimatums, guns had all proved useless. Already an unwelcome price was being paid in casualties and damaged ships. And as the operation continued, the fighting and the losses could only escalate—almost certainly to no purpose. Dakar's defenders seemed determined not to give in, and appeared perfectly capable of continuing their resistance. Now, in the minds of the commanders was the crucial question: Should Menace be abandoned?

'It was clear enough,' Spears noted, 'the commanders felt the job was beyond their strength. Admiral spoke of insoluble problem of battleship versus land battery. It was clear that he would like to get out of it, but de Gaulle, rightly, I think, insisted in view of tone of ultimatum that it was too much of a knock to just slink away. Both commanders were anxious to know what the effect on moral of people of Dakar would be because of bombardment. De Gaulle thought it certainly must have antagonized them. Irwin thought a landing under present conditions, with fleet free to come out, was a desperate enterprise, and with this de Gaulle agreed. De Gaulle very much opposed to complete breaking off of action as, in view of ultimatum, this could be taken as nothing less than an acknowledgement of complete and utter failure. Suggested a face-saving device that Dakar should be informed that bombardment had ceased at his request. Urged, however, that blockade should not merely be a commercial one, as previously, but that the ships should be kept in harbour, if possible, or at least prevented from going south.'[8]

All through the conference, de Gaulle chain-smoked. Cunningham watched with increasing anxiety as he tossed his burning cigarette ends into the bridge's wooden gratings. At last the admiral propelled an empty shell case towards him for use as an ashtray. When de Gaulle missed this one, others were pushed in his direction, while, as Spears records, 'the distressed admiral watched the cigarette ends in flight with the hypnotized attention of a Wimbledon fan following a champion's service.'[9]

'No doubt,' Spears continues, 'that situation at Dakar has very much changed owing to what must have been immense pressure from Vichy. Air Force, as well as Navy, seem to be both determined and aggressive. De Gaulle was extremely pre-occupied with what action of French may be. He was most anxious that it should be made clear that Dakar troops had fired first, which is certainly the case. Admiral told me that we had suffered casualties in fleet before we returned fire, and the Free French ships and *fusiliers marins*, as well as the envoys, were fired at long before any action on our part . . . We left the second the conference was over.'[10]

According to de Gaulle's version of the meeting, he told Cunningham that bombardment would decide nothing. A landing against opposition would, he stressed, lead to a pitched battle which he wished to avoid and whose outcome would be very doubtful. He therefore advocated giving up any present idea of taking Dakar. As an alternative he proposed a landing at St Louis, for example, a point from which Dakar could be reached by an advance overland. 'The British admiral and general fell in with my view regarding the immediate future,' de Gaulle recorded.[11]

The general's disillusionment at the collapse of his plans was plain to all. 'He was deeply distressed,' it was noted, 'and expressed himself as being surprised at the nature of the defences, which were much superior to anything he had expected . . . He blamed himself for undue optimism as to the support from Dakar and the strength of the defence.' But one man present recorded with admiration: 'His attitude when he was naturally suffering from the terrible disappointment which his reception [at Dakar] undoubtedly gave him was that of a great man.'[12]

De Gaulle and Spears returned to the *Westernland* under the firm impression that Cunningham and Irwin were ready to recommend the cancellation of Menace. 'The commanders are going to signal to London,' he wrote. 'It will be bitter for Winston, who told them to capture Dakar in a signal received last night or this morning.'[13]

Cunningham had been much discouraged by the failure of his battleships to knock out Dakar's coast batteries. The problem of naval guns versus shore-based artillery was an old one. Nelson had recognized the superiority of coast guns at shorter ranges, though naval guns might redress this disadvantage by out-ranging the shore batteries and firing their larger-calibre shells. But in this instance Cunningham had to reckon with the *Richelieu*, whose 15-inch salvoes were as effective, for range and weight, as anything he could deliver. His shooting was further hindered by smoke-screens and the activity of French planes which prevented accurate observation. He had, however, another weapon: the air arm. And this he had decided to send in again. Even while the Menace leaders were closeted on the *Barham*, an attack by torpedo-carrying planes was being mounted, on his orders, from the *Ark Royal*. Their specific target was the French warships which were not only protecting the shore batteries but posed a continuing threat to his slow-moving, vulnerable transports. Unless these were neutralized, no shred of hope remained for Operation Menace.

Feeling on the *Ark Royal* had been unhappy since the reverses of the previous day. Officers and crew were bewildered at the violent opposition being shown by their recent allies. And the reaction of the Free French had been positively angry. Any scruples they may have had about fighting fellow-Frenchmen had vanished, and they were bitterly lamenting that their Foreign Legion contingent had not been landed at Rufisque. Before that morning's actions one Frenchman had been heard consigning Admiral Landriau to the gallows. Another was seen to pat a 500-lb bomb being loaded on to a Skua, jesting that it would make the admiral a nice breakfast. But these actions had signally failed to achieve success, and cost four British planes. Now the orders for this new attack brought the *Ark Royal* fresh hopes that the failure might be redeemed with the knocking-out of the main prop of Dakar's defences.

But these hopes were to be rudely shattered. The attack, by nine Swordfish with three Skua escorts, was launched around 3.30: its main target the Vichy cruisers. As the planes flew in at zero height they were met by blazing anti-aircraft fire from the cruisers and two were quickly shot down. This left only one section of three planes in effective formation. Pressing home their assault they fired their three torpedoes. But all ploughed harmlessly across the waters of the roadstead, the nearest miss passing between the *Georges Leygues* and *Montcalm* some 70 yards from the latter's stern. The surviving planes regained the *Ark Royal*, to report another failure. In the laconic words of an *Ark Royal* officer: 'This ended another unsatisfactory day.'[14]

The previous evening at Vichy, Paul Baudouin had told press correspondents: 'Wounded as she may be, France is still capable of defending herself and giving blow for blow.' She was already demonstrating this at Dakar itself, but Baudouin was warning Britain that France could strike back nearer home.

Now, on the 24th (in accordance with Vichy's decision of the day before), a sharp reprisal raid was launched against Gibraltar. Some 40 French bombers from Algiers flew over the Rock, dropping about 150 bombs with little damage. They met considerable ack-ack fire but no fighter opposition, and retired without loss. But was the Gibraltar raid a prelude to war between France and Britain? For those who feared that the Dakar operation (following the Mers-el-Kebir episode and the earlier Dakar raid on the *Richelieu*) might push Vichy into declaring war, Baudouin had reassuring words. The British action was not a *casus belli*, he declared.[15]

Indeed, on this day at Vichy, French anger at the Dakar attack was being tempered by a cautious satisfaction. Not only was the attempt going badly for the British, but Ministers realized that they might turn it to their advantage *vis-à-vis* their German masters. At a morning Cabinet attended by Pétain, Laval, Huntziger, Darlan, Bergeret and Baudouin, Laval was briefed on the line he should take at a meeting he was having with the Germans in Paris later that day. He was to ask that France be granted every facility for organising a strong defence of her colonies; and further, that France be allowed to make a declaration that she had received assurances from Germany that France's West African colonies would never be occupied by Germany during the armistice period, nor would they be affected by a peace treaty. This, the Ministers calculated, would enable them to make an effective reply to the British propaganda charges that the Germans were planning to take over Dakar.[16]

To mark France's determination to defend her possessions, the Ministers were told, orders had been given—without waiting for permission from the German and Italian Armistice Commissions, the normal authorizing bodies—for the rearming of the battleship *Strasbourg* and a number of cruisers at Toulon. This news had reached de Gaulle and Spears on the *Westernland* and added to their worries. Spears even feared that the warships were making for Dakar. 'Heavy reinforcements may also be on the way by air,' he predicted.[17]

But far from the troubled scene of Dakar it was easier to remain unruffled. At Geneva that day the Frenchman Louis Rougier, an emissary of Pétain on his way to England to make an approach to Churchill, warned the British Consul-General that the Dakar attack would damage Anglo-French relations. 'I admired the perfect self-assurance,' Rougier noted, 'with which he answered me: "The British Admiralty doesn't undertake anything lightly."' Two days later, to Rougier's gratification, the Consul-General asked his permission to telegraph his warning to the Foreign Office.[18]

Back on the *Westernland* after the *Barham* meeting, de Gaulle gave vent to his despondency. He talked to Spears in the darkness of the captain's bridge. '"That there is a complete failure, none can deny," he said . . . "It must be faced up to. It is difficult to size up how things will go. What will the reaction of Frenchmen of France be? I must not be a man who can be described as one who fights Frenchmen. My own people could turn on me. Men like Larminat may be critical, say I should have worked progressively rather than go bald-headed for Dakar first of all".'

'De Gaulle said that to carry out small operations would have no effect now, and be very difficult in Senegal where the pro-Vichy leaders would now have it all their own way. His conclusion is that the only way to save himself from the accusation of fighting Frenchmen is to go and fight where he can. After parading his men at Duala, he would take them to Egypt and fight the Italians there. He spoke even, if opinion turned against him, of handing over to General Catroux [the ex-Governor-General of Indo-China who was offering de Gaulle his services].'[19]

De Gaulle's talk of Egypt left Spears highly uneasy. He thought that if he went there as a little-known figure, unable to obtain recruits except possibly from Syria, 'he would cease to exist.' On the other hand, by staying in Africa he could consolidate his position and continue to threaten the Vichy authorities in Senegal. 'Here,' Spears wrote, 'he has an embryo Empire. To go to Egypt means he is . . . throwing in the sponge.'[20]

But whatever course de Gaulle now decided on, he was clear

147

about one thing. Operation Menace must be called off. This
was stressed in a cipher message from the Spears Mission to
General Ismay in London, for transmission to the Prime Minister, sent at 9 o'clock that night:

'De Gaulle agrees with commanders it would be unwise to
attempt landing now in face unexpectedly determined opposition. Nature of opposition unexpected and seems due to tremendous effort by Vichy . . . De Gaulle suggested as good
face-saving device that Dakar should be informed bombardment
should cease at his request . . . He thinks movements of ships
at least southwards should be prevented. De Gaulle wants to go
to Bathurst with his force (a) to exercise the men who have not
been ashore since England; (b) to obtain information on real
conditions in Senegal . . .'[21]

But, on the *Barham*, the commanders themselves had now had
second thoughts about abandoning Menace. After the departure
of de Gaulle and Spears they had discussed the matter further
and resolved to make one more effort. As Irwin put it, 'We
decided to have another crack.' They had already cabled the
Admiralty, at 2.15 pm, with a discouraging report on the prospects of taking Dakar. Now, at 7.30, they signalled again, reporting that a landing was not practicable in face of the existing
difficulties and that the alternatives were to withdraw immediately or continue the bombardment; they proposed however to
renew the bombardment next day and if this failed they recommended the adoption of de Gaulle's proposal to break off.[22]

After two days of ineffective shelling, with Dakar's forts and
warships still virtually intact, another naval bombardment promised to be just a waste of ammunition. Moreover there was
high risk of further casualty and damage to Cunningham's
force. And while the defences remained undestroyed a landing
was out of the question. Yet the alternative—a withdrawal and
return to Freetown—would be plain and obvious defeat. This
was the bleak situation facing Cunningham and Irwin as the
Anglo-French armada waited uncertainly off the African coast
on the night of the 24th.

In the Vichy warships, by contrast, the mood was buoyant.

After the day's successful resistance the crews were said to be 'choc-a-bloc with pride' and unworried, even eager, at the prospect of another British attack. The cruisers were little damaged. 'Their apparatus and material have behaved wonderfully,' it was recorded. 'The engineers have surpassed themselves. In spite of the constant manoeuvring and the jarring inflicted on the engines, not the slightest damage had been reported. In the turrets the chief gunners are cleaning out their guns for what one of them calls "Tomorrow morning's birthday", because the 25th September will be the decisive day in the attack on Dakar.'

CHAPTER XII

MENACE DAY THREE—DISASTER

In Downing Street, London, Winston Churchill faced an even heavier problem than the Menace commanders. For him Dakar was not just a military matter but a highly sensitive political one. The abandonment of Menace, as foreshadowed in the latest reports from the British leaders and de Gaulle, would not only be hailed as a resounding victory by Vichy and Berlin, but cause acute dismay in Washington. In sponsoring the operation Churchill had counted heavily on the moral support of President Roosevelt, stressing the strategic importance of Dakar to the United States as well as Britain. On the 23rd, as Menace was being launched, he had been cheered to receive a cable from Roosevelt expressing his approval of the operation. In a grateful reply he had re-emphasized the joint Anglo-American interest in preserving Dakar from German occupation, and added: 'It looks as if there might be a stiff fight. Perhaps not, but anyhow orders have been given to ram it through.'[1] Now, less than two days later, he might shortly have to tell Roosevelt that Operation Menace had failed. At this critical moment, when it was vital for Britain to impress America with her fighting capacity and determination in order to obtain the maximum possible aid towards continuing the war, such a failure could prove a sharp setback to Anglo-American relations.

The deepening Dakar crisis had been urgently occupying Ministers and service chiefs since the previous evening. But the time-lag between the dispatch of Cunningham's signals and their presentation in London had further confused an already somewhat obscure situation. The signal sent at 2.15 on the 24th —putting in doubt the feasibility of continuing Menace—had reached the Admiralty at 6.50 pm. But the one sent at 7.30— proposing a renewal of the bombardment, and cancellation in the event of failure—arrived only at 5.10 am on the 25th. The first was considered at a meeting of the Defence Committee late on the 24th, and in reply Cunningham was asked for full details of the position. But to this Churchill, too, sent off his own irascible rejoinder just after midnight: 'Your signal gives no indication of your plans. We asked you particularly to be full and clear in your accounts. Why have you not sent two or three hundred words to let us know your difficulties and how you propose to meet them? . . . Pray act as you think best, meanwhile give reasoned answer to these points. Matter must be pushed to conclusion without delay.'[2]

Understandably this was not appreciated by Cunningham. The bizarre request for a few hundred words to be sent off in the midst of his handling of a complex and increasingly difficult situation made the tired and overworked admiral—as Captain Walter, his CSO, recalls—'very shirty'. Sitting up with Irwin through the hot and sticky night he did however answer the previous request for more information. This outlined the current gloomy situation and said that the Joint Commanders would continue the operation and make a landing if it proved possible. (Written at 3.44 am on the 25th, this cable was to be considered by the Defence Committee at a 10 am meeting on the 25th along with that sent at 7.30 pm on the 24th.)

On the *Westernland*, meanwhile, de Gaulle and Spears had gone to bed on the previous night fully believing that Menace was 'off'. They were therefore astonished to receive a signal from the *Barham* early on the 25th that it was 'on' again. As Spears notes, this 'indicated that, on fresh information, they [the commanders] had altered the point of view they had expressed at the conference in the *Barham*.' Spears guessed that their decision had been influenced by Churchill's 'stop at nothing' order, though the commanders themselves gave as a reason an air report that Dakar's defences were more seriously damaged that was previously thought. De Gaulle, on learning the news, was decidedly offended that the commanders should have changed their minds without first consulting him.

But the commanders had considered all the factors and made their uneasy choice. And in what was now a desperate bid to break the French defences, Operation Menace entered its third day.

Between 4 and 5 am the Vichy cruisers had left harbour to resume their evasion tactics of the day before. An air patrol from the *Ark Royal* flying over Dakar at dawn reported the cruisers in the outer roads and the destroyers ready to lay a smoke-screen. At her berth in the harbour the *Richelieu* was seen attached by the stern to a tug so that she could be towed into position to use her 15-inch guns. But for Cunningham there was one hopeful omen. Overnight the last traces of fog had gone and now, under clear skies and a bright sun, visibility was unlimited. At long last his guns would have the chance of being used effectively.

Cunningham's Order of the Day was terse and to the point: the object was 'finally to compass the destruction of the French warships.' This would be carried out by naval bombardment alone: aircraft would not be employed except for spotting and observation. But the first gunfire was from an ack-ack battery on the *Richelieu* which, shortly before seven, brought down an English reconnaissance plane. Under the mounting sun the shore lookouts scanned the empty horizon for sight of the British force. But it was a French air patrol that first spotted it around 7.30, steaming up from the south. Ten minutes later Cap Manuel reported two large ships—the *Barham* and the *Resolution*—far to the south-east. A general alert was sounded, and the *Richelieu* prepared to engage the battleships. The *Georges Leygues* and the *Montcalm* would deal with the British cruisers which had appeared soon after, steaming just east of the battleships.

In clear visibility, the range closed to 22,000 yards. Cunningham's force turned parallel to the shore to bring its guns to bear. Then, at 9 o'clock, pandemonium was loosed as the French and British opened fire almost together. The Gorée batteries joined in, firing at the cruisers. Once again the British shooting was hampered by a dense smoke-screen from the destroyers that hid the town and harbour. And once more the French cruisers in the outer roads, girdled by shell-bursts, escaped unscathed. The *Richelieu*, however, was less lucky. At the very start of the action a 15-inch shell tore into her, a direct hit from the *Barham*, whose spotting was being directed by one of her Walrus planes. Flames spurted up, to be soon extinguished—and the Walrus was quickly brought down. But almost simultaneously with the hit on the *Richelieu* Cunningham's force itself suffered a major calamity.

Lurking in wait for the British battleships since dawn had been the third and last of Dakar's submarine flotilla, the *Beveziers*. She had been ordered into position as a result of shrewd thinking by Admiral Landriau, who had calculated that the battleships would again approach Dakar on the same course as on the 24th (a manoeuvre to avoid two important shore batteries). Landriau had assumed correctly. Around 8 o'clock the *Beveziers'* periscope picked up the battleships, with their destroyer escorts, steaming at 20 knots. For an hour the submarine shadowed them, ready to attack. Then, at a point eight miles off Cap Manuel, the chance came. Though herself detected by the destroyers and under attack from depth-charges, she loosed five torpedoes at the *Resolution* at a range of 2,500 yards. A plane from the *Ark Royal* on anti-submarine patrol spotted the tell-tale track and warned the *Resolution*, but too late. The first four torpedoes missed but the fifth struck her amidships just forward of the funnel.

There was a dull explosion. A huge spout of water rose against the *Resolution*'s grey hull and her firing ceased abruptly. Belching black smoke, listing heavily to port and down by the bows, she slowed and stopped. The crews on the nearby warships watched in consternation as she drifted helplessly. An officer on the destroyer *Dragon*, attending the transports nine miles away to the south, observed the scene through binoculars.

He saw the crippled vessel, steam billowing from her funnel, being surrounded by the *Barham, Cumberland, Cornwall* and several destroyers—which seemed 'like footballers watching a stricken team-mate.'[3] 'The torpedo's explosion seemed to echo round the fleet like a command to cease fire,' noted another watcher.[4] For Cunningham the hit on the *Resolution* spelt disaster, for the loss of her formidable fire-power left his force outgunned by the Dakar defenders. But there was more trouble to come. Two shells crashed into the cruiser *Australia*, and the *Barham* herself was struck in the bows by a round from the *Richelieu*. The damage was not serious, far less so than the blow to an already badly shaken morale.

Dakar was throwing in everything it could against Cunningham's force—bombs as well as shells and torpedoes. Harassed by French bombers from Ouakam, Cunningham proposed to the *Ark Royal*'s captain that a counter-strike be mounted on Ouakam airfield. But this met with no favour. A daylight attack by his old and slow Swordfish planes would, the captain explained, be costly and ineffectual. In the circumstances there was nothing for it: less than 30 minutes after the start of the action Cunningham ordered a cease-fire.

As the guns stopped and the fleet turned seawards, Cunningham and Irwin now faced the crucial question whether to resume or break off the engagement altogether. After this disastrous opening it seemed useless to continue. But before making the final decision they weighed the pros and cons—as the record shows—with painstaking care. They concluded that the chance of achieving the original object, the taking of Dakar, was remote; and that the prospect of destroying the *Richelieu* and the two Toulon cruisers without incurring disproportionate damage to the *Barham, Devonshire* and *Australia* now appeared improbable, owing to (i) the poor shooting of the *Barham* (this being due to fighter interference with spotting accuracy and the newly commissioned state of the battleship), (ii) smoke-screening of targets, and (iii) accuracy of enemy fire. They noted the presence of at least one other submarine in the vicinity, the increasing air opposition, and the possibility of enemy ammunition being nearly exhausted was not confirmed. They further studied the likely effect on the British war effort of the probable loss of, or damage to, a second capital ship for comparatively small result; and on the other hand the effect on Britain's world prestige of the admission of failure to implement the threat to Dakar. But for the two commanders the conclusion was virtually foregone. 'After considering all these points,' reported Cunningham, 'I decided to withdraw the force.'[5]

Soon after, the Joint Commanders' signal flashed from the *Barham* to the Admiralty in London, reporting the morning's catastrophic action and recommending the withdrawal of Cunningham's force.

In Dakar's harbour and outer roads, the French crews were jubilantly hailing the morning's success. The crippling of the *Resolution* was a particular triumph, for it was the *Resolution* that had destroyed the battleship *Bretagne* at Mers-el-Kebir. The cruiser *Montcalm*, passing the *Georges Leygues* in the roads, signalled 'How goes it?' '*Au poil* (Bang on)!' answered the *Georges Leygues*. And the *Beveziers*, shaken by depth-charges but undamaged, returned to Dakar harbour soon after 11 to be greeted by cheering sailors.

The British transports, circling off-shore ten miles south of Dakar, had been well away from the battle. Their troops had been waiting since dawn, prepared to go into action. For almost all of them, indeed, the whole operation had been a matter of waiting. On the *Ettrick* it was believed that if the bombardment failed to bring about a surrender, the long-expected landing would be made at last. Once the *Ettrick*'s troops had paraded ready to embark on the landing craft, but then they were stood down. Soon after came the news that Menace was 'off'; and the *Ettrick* started moving at full speed out to sea. Cunningham's squadron appeared, and with a shock watchers saw the crippled *Resolution*. 'We could see her being taken in tow,' recorded Lieutenant St John, 'heeled over to port, her great guns pointing to starboard to stop her turning turtle.'[6]

On the *Westernland*, too, there was anxious waiting. 'We were without news,' noted Spears, 'when we were ordered—late in the morning—to steam full speed southwards. It was agonizing, as the bombardment was to have started at six (sic).' De Gaulle, already annoyed that the commanders had not consulted him before renewing the attack, was rapidly losing patience. Soon after noon he signalled Cunningham saying he knew nothing and asking why the convoy was sailing southwards. Back came the terse reply: the morning's action 'had confirmed the effectiveness of the defences.' Cunningham added that the Government had been asked to adopt de Gaulle's proposals of the 24th, that is to go to Bathurst with a view to planning a land attack on Dakar, and that meanwhile he was steaming all ships southwards. He asked de Gaulle to conform until a decision on his proposals had been received from the Government.[7]

Exactly how de Gaulle thought he could win Dakar by a land attack, using only Free French troops, is not clear. The failure of Operation Menace, powerfully backed by the British, was indication enough that the port would not fall to his forces alone. But Dakar, and all that its capture implied for himself and the Free French movement, had become an obsession with de Gaulle. And now this morning, even though his radio appeals to Dakar over the last two days had proved so fruitless, from the wireless cabin in the *Westernland* he beamed one more impassioned call to them:

'The men of Vichy who are unwilling to fight the invaders are not afraid to launch civil war by firing on General de Gaulle's envoys and soldiers. At the present moment these same men are consigning Dakar to destruction. Before this destruction starts, General de Gaulle once more adjures with all his heart the Frenchmen of Dakar to join without delay to drive out these evil leaders and resume the good fight for the liberation of France!'[8]

It was a forlorn appeal. After the gunfire and the bloodshed and in the face of the obvious ascendancy of the pro-Vichy forces, prospects of his enlisting recruits to his standard were never poorer.

In Britain the public—if it could pay much attention to anything beyond Hitler's bombing and the still imminent threat of invasion—was now learning something about the 'reasons' for the Daker operation. On the 25th the diplomatic correspondent of *The Times* reported as follows: 'There had for some time been evidence that the Germans were planning to establish control at Dakar . . . German and Italian staff officers had been flying there under various pretexts. At the same time there had been evidence . . . that many Frenchmen in the town were anxious to join the cause of Free France. Probably because the strength of this healthy movement had become known to Vichy (as well as Berlin and Rome), the Vichy Government . . . had lately sent three cruisers and three destroyers to add to the defensive strength of the fortress there. An Allied force, naval, air, and military, was in the vicinity . . .' But the news reports contained no hint of Menace's likely or impending failure. Headlines in *The Times* announced 'Dakar Action Continues; Vichy Calls for Assistance; De Gaulle's Envoys Fired on.'[9]

But in Whitehall the previous day's news had prepared Churchill and his colleagues for the worst. The Defence Committee, meeting at 10 am, had before it Cunningham's two cables timed at 7.30 pm on the 24th and 3.44 am on the 25th (the first proposing a renewal of bombardment on the 25th and a withdrawal in the event of failure, and the second saying the operation would be continued and a landing made if possible). For the committee the purport of these was grave enough for the conclusion that 'no pressure should be brought to bear on the commanders to take any action against their better judgment.' Ninety minutes later the War Cabinet met. Studying Cunningham's latest reports and the Defence Committee's conclusion on them, the War Cabinet's decision might have been inevitable in any case. But these reports were already out of date. And even as they were being studied, Cunningham's latest signal arrived in the Cabinet Room, reporting that morning's action. With its announcement of the loss of the *Resolution* and the commanders' recommendation to withdraw, it was the crowning blow in the tale of disaster.[10]

A tense and anxious discussion followed. Churchill submitted that two courses for Menace were open: to let the commanders attempt a landing, or to abandon the operation. In his view a landing was now ruled out by the loss of the *Resolution*. As for the second course, he pointed out that Dakar had undoubtedly been strengthened by the arrival of the Vichy cruisers with their determined officers; and not only would a landing run the risk of being cut off, but the naval force, if it remained in support off Dakar, might well be exposed to U-boat attack. Attlee thought Menace had been a 'justifiable gamble'. Halifax suggested that too much reliance had been put on the optimistic forecasts of de Gaulle's supporters. Alexander, the First Lord of the Admiralty, confessed that though opposed to the expedition from the start, he would—once it had begun—have favoured its continuation, had it not been for the loss of the *Resolution*.[11]

'It seemed clear that the matter had been pressed as far as prudence and our resources would allow,' Churchill wrote later. 'We therefore were all agreed to push no more.' He left the Cabinet Room to draft a signal to the Menace commanders: 'On all the information now before us, including damage to *Resolution*, we have decided that the enterprise against Dakar should be abandoned . . . Unless something has happened which we do not know, which makes you wish to attempt landing in force, you should forthwith break off. You should inform us "Most Immediate" whether you concur . . .' The message continued that, on the abandonment of Menace, efforts would be made to provide a naval cover for Duala, but that de Gaulle could not be safeguarded if he remained at Bathurst.

The signal was approved by the War Cabinet and sent out at 1.27 pm. Shortly the commanders' reply came back: 'Concur in breaking off.'[12] The seal had been put to what was already a *fait accompli*.

Churchill had another signal to send, too—a signal that cost him much to write. It was addressed 'Former Naval Person to President Roosevelt' and ran: 'I much regret we had to abandon Dakar enterprise. Vichy got in before us and animated defence with partisans and gunnery experts. All friendly elements were gripped and held down. Several of our ships were hit, and to persist with landing in force would have tied us to an undue commitment, when you think of what we have on our hands already.'[13]

As the British squadron steamed away from Dakar, the weary French gun-crews ashore and afloat stood down, elated by victory. 'There was no more question of Dakar being destroyed,' recorded a writer. 'The affair was over.' But the commanders were taking no chances. The Vichy cruisers were to remain at the ready in the outer roads till the 27th, and a strict air watch was kept up. Meanwhile the crews on the merchantmen resigned themselves to gloom. They listened to the jubilant radio announcements from Berlin and Vichy and contrasted them with the silence from London. For three days they had been in the thick of it, suffering damage and casualties from British guns, and all for nothing. Now it was clear that any further Allied attempt on Dakar in the near future was ruled out, and they would have to stay holed up in this steamy port indefinitely. And on the evening of the 25th there was an added blow for the Norwegians: the news that the pro-German Vidkun Quisling had assumed executive power in Norway.

Meanwhile Vichy was keeping up her reprisal raids on Gibraltar. On the night of the 24th–25th a 'demonstration' naval foray was staged by four destroyers from Casablanca, and on the 25th over 100 planes bombed the Rock, causing some damage at the cost of two aircraft down. The actions were as much to show Germany that France could handle attacks on her possessions without German intervention as to warn Britain against repeating such attacks. But there was no doubt about Vichy's anger at the Dakar assault. On the morning of the 25th Baudouin sent the Vichy Ambassador in Madrid a telegram for Sir Samuel Hoare in which he stressed that the attempt on Dakar was 'cold, premeditated and wholly inexcusable aggression.'[14]

'Some days before the attack on Dakar,' Baudouin continued,

'the English admiral commanding in the Atlantic told the French admiral not to put in at Dakar as it was in German hands. This statement was entirely untrue as there was neither a German at Dakar nor a German ship anywhere in the colony. . . . From the standpoint of general politics, there has been a general improvement in Franco-British relations during the past weeks. You [Sir Samuel Hoare] are yourself in an excellent position to bear witness to this. The achievement confers real merit on us, taking into account the previous attitude of Great Britain where we were concerned, and our perseverance, as your files show. I cannot understand what advantage England hopes to gain by upsetting this state of affairs. It can be said of her aggression that it was worse than a crime—it was a blunder.'[15]

That evening Baudouin received General Weygand, who told him he was shortly going to North Africa. They discussed the Dakar affair at length, and Weygand said he was both sorry and glad at not having been at Dakar; for had he been there he might have been obliged to shoot the emissary of de Gaulle, and that emissary was the grandson of Marshal Foch!'[16]*

In the bright afternoon sun the Menace armada headed south for Freetown, its business over. Ahead sailed the transports, and ten miles astern the warships, acting as a rearguard. Everywhere, varying with the extent to which officers and men had been involved, was a sense of let-down, frustration, defeat. On the *Barham*, among the combined staff who had toiled over three days to direct and handle the operation, there was too a mood of sheer physical relief that it was ended. Working conditions had been even more diabolical than on the *Devonshire*. And at night, in the heat, sleep in the cabins was almost impossible. Some officers even slept in chairs in the ward-room. Worse still, something had gone wrong with the hot water system, so that water served with drinks was not merely warm but about the temperature of a hot cup of tea. The clerical staff suffered no less.

* The envoy in question was Captain Bécourt de Foch. Weygand's feelings were explained by the fact that Marshal Foch, under whom he had served in the First World War, was one of his greatest heroes.

Throughout the three days their only meals consisted of sand-wiches of bully beef which was so hot that it melted and, on the last day, 'so old that it stank.'[17] With such handicaps it was a wonder that the staff functioned as well as it did. The fact that the *Barham* was a newly commissioned ship may have been partly responsible. But what was really needed for such operations—as Irwin was later to urge so strongly—was a properly appointed Headquarters Ship.

On the *Westernland* de Gaulle was tasting the bitterness of failure and anxiously considering his next move. But his most urgent concern was how to present the operation to the public. The Dakar *débâcle* was likely to be as damaging a blow to his prestige with the British and Free French as it was to him per-sonally. He had to put the case in a way that justified him in starting the operation and accounted for its collapse through no fault of his own. He thereupon produced a version which he hopefully believed would vindicate himself and disarm critics.

He cabled this forthwith to General Ismay in London. It explained that a large section of the population had requested his presence; that it was known that the Germans intended to occupy Dakar; that, in answer to the call of his supporters, he had resolved to present himself before Dakar and request the authorities, the garrison and the population to rally to him; that the Vichy Government was resolved, on German orders, to break the Free French movement. The explanation continued that his approaches were rebuffed and fire was opened on the envoys and then on the planes and ships. The Rufisque landing attempt was repulsed with casualties. De Gaulle, not wishing to engage French troops, then withdrew his forces, and the British fleet ceased the attack at his express request.[18]

Spears had never seen the general so shattered and indecisive. 'This worried me,' he noted that day. 'He is brave, but is more of a gambler than a resolute man, it turns out. For the moment he cannot see his way.' As the convoy ploughed southwards, de Gaulle spent the afternoon toying first with one unlikely plan and then another. 'To begin with he proposed making straight for Konakri,' Spears recounted, 'and I cheered (having urged refusal to accept defeat). De Gaulle or rather I sent the commanders a signal to this effect. De Gaulle then sent for the paper giving the strength of the garrison at Konakri, and it was undoubtedly very strong.'[19]

'This led him to the conclusion,' the Official Mission report adds, 'that he would have to face possible very strong opposition if he attempted a forced landing . . . De Gaulle becoming increasingly opposed to idea of engaging his forces against Frenchmen and is worrying more and more as to what the effect on public opinion in France and among his own supporters may be if he creates such a situation. Opinion of troops on board undoubtedly is that they are infuriated at having been fired at and would not in the least mind tackling those Frenchmen who have caused them losses. But it cannot be denied that de Gaulle is entitled to fear accusation of provoking civil war. He therefore suggested landing his forces at Freetown, where it is essential to allow them to land . . . and consulting his emissaries.

'All afternoon and evening de Gaulle's mind was straying more and more to sending his troops to Egypt, believing that to fight the Italians there would counteract bad impression of Dakar. Disadvantage of this is that if Equatorial Africa feels itself abandoned it would probably revert to Vichy, and he himself would cease to be the important figurehead he has become should he be a mere commander of a small force in Egypt.'[20]

Spears had his own doubts and worries too. 'I am sad to think of this flat failure and that I pressed for the expedition,' he records. 'I imagine what will be said of my telegram from Freetown urging action. I cannot imagine how I shall dispose or arrange the Mission, or what use it will be, or what I can do best. The *Resolution* business is a nightmare.' He regretted that his proposal for a personal approach to Dakar's Governor-General had been refused by the commanders: 'My landing would perhaps have made no difference, but I could at least have tried to get an interview for de Gaulle, possibly on neutral ground, suggested that the Governor should come but on one of his warships. The great thing was to establish contact.'

As darkness fell over the convoy, Spears closed that day's

diary on a dismal note: 'The heat is great. You sit and sweat, and by night the heat is terrific owing to the blackout. Everything closed, no air, no fans . . .'[21]

CHAPTER XIII

AFTERMATH

By the 27th September the Menace convoy had trailed back to Freetown. Stretched across the glassy waters of the harbour, the warships and transports stood idle in the humid heat. Amidst them the *Resolution*, towed back from Dakar by the *Barham*, 'lay looking like a dead whale.'[1] The crippled battleship—she would take months to repair—symbolized the extent of the reverse suffered by the Royal Navy and indeed by the entire Menace project. Apart from the *Resolution*, varying damage had been caused to the *Barham*, *Cumberland*, *Australia*, *Dragon*, *Inglefield*, *Foresight*, *Fury* and *Delhi*, and at least 12 planes had been lost. Casualties thankfully were small.

All this was hardly worse than the damage sustained by the French: two submarines sunk, two destroyers burnt out and the already damaged *Richelieu* hit by a 15-inch shell. And the French casualties, reputedly some 500 killed and wounded (including civilians), were far greater than those of the Allies. But the real reading of the balance sheet was in the total failure of Menace to achieve its aim. De Gaulle's envoys had been sent packing, the Rufisque landing attempt had been a fiasco, the expected support within Dakar had not materialized, and the Navy's guns had signally failed to break the defences.

Throughout the convoy ran a feeling of bafflement and anti-climax. 'Operation Menace—I call it Operation Muddle!' declared a dejected *Ark Royal* pilot.[2] On the *Westernland* the sense of defeat was heavy. De Gaulle brooded in his cabin, seized by a black depression. 'The days which followed the Dakar defeat were cruel for me,' he wrote. He confessed to feeling like someone whose house had been shaken by an earthquake.[3] 'After Dakar,' said one associate, 'he was never the same man.' It was reported he even contemplated suicide. Well aware what the cost of the failure would be to himself and the Free French movement, he was searching desperately for some way to redeem it. En route to Freetown 'he still argued endlessly about taking his troops to Egypt,' Spears noted.[4] One consoling message reached him during the voyage from Colonel Leclerc, now in control of the French Cameroons: 'The Cameroons is ready to respond to your call whatever happens.'

But his satisfaction was damped by a cable he received at Freetown on the 27th. Addressed to New York by an American correspondent in London, it ran: '. . . One result of what is admitted here to be a blow to British prestige may be the ousting of General de Gaulle as leader of the Free French movement. A British *communiqué* emphasized that it had been his idea to send the expedition and that he had miscalculated the support he had received there. French circles in London were also questioning his political judgment and the advisability of keeping him as leader . . .'[5]

The attacks—all too expected—had begun. But this challenge to his leadership was a sore affront. Despite the Dakar fiasco, de Gaulle still saw himself as France's appointed leader, the man of destiny who alone could rescue her from defeat. It was only a matter of accepting one reverse and trying again wherever the chance offered. He knew he had the support of his troops at Freetown. Immediately on arrival there he had inspected his ships and found the men eager to carry on. And that same day, pondering his next moves, he saw some light in the darkness. He cabled hopefully to his chief lieutenants in Africa, Larminat and Leclerc, and Governor Eboué at Fort Lamy. His present scheme he said, was to come with his troops, ships and planes to French Equatorial Africa, and from there to extend the Free French Empire towards Dakar and send the troops to fight the Italians. He prescribed the attitude to be followed: 'Free Frenchmen won the first round in Africa and Oceania. The Germans, using Vichy as a catspaw, won the second round at Dakar. The match continues. There are very favourable indications in France, in Syria and North Africa and the West Indies. Hope to see you soon.'[6]

De Gaulle's immediate future was a problem not only for himself but for the British Government. The British could no longer spare any naval force to aid him on some further African adventure. The most that could be done was to provide an escort for his transports to Duala or some similar destination. Moreover, because of the Dakar failure de Gaulle was now a political liability whose continued backing would be an acute embarrassment. Henceforth he would have to act on his own. The best way he could redeem his shattered credit was by registering some success without British help. During a talk with him on the *Westernland*, Spears told him: 'I don't believe Dakar can have done any harm that cannot be retrieved, and will be on the first occasion.' 'But I took advantage of the position,' Spears added, 'to urge the importance of an immediate success, i.e. the taking of Libreville.'[7]

De Gaulle certainly had much to retrieve. The news of Menace's failure had produced fierce and bitter condemnation in both London and Washington. In the press and elsewhere there were attacks on the British Foreign Office, Churchill and, most violent of all, on de Gaulle. The distrust and suspicion of him that had previously simmered in various quarters on both sides of the Atlantic now burst into the open. De Gaulle, it was asserted, was responsible for the whole scheme, virtually forcing his ideas on Churchill and the Menace commanders. Moreover, it was the Free French in England who had jeopardised it by their careless talk beforehand. De Gaulle, it was now said, was no longer to be trusted as the Free French leader and should be replaced by Catroux or Muselier. In Roosevelt's view the Dakar failure showed de Gaulle as a dangerous meddler whose precipitate action gravely damaged Anglo-Vichy relations and risked bringing Hitler into the Mediterranean or even the

Atlantic, thus breaching a firm principle of American policy and imperilling American security.

Criticism fell hard on Churchill himself. One of his strongest assailants was Robert Menzies, Australia's Prime Minister. On the 29th September Menzies cabled him: 'We are very disturbed in regard to Dakar incident . . . It is difficult to understand why attempt was made unless overwhelming chances of success. To make what appears at this distance to be a half-hearted attack is to incur a damaging loss of prestige . . .' Churchill replied, stressing that the situation at Dakar was radically changed by the arrival of the French cruisers at Dakar with Vichy supporters, and by the manning of the batteries by hostile naval personnel. He explained that the Joint Commanders, after earlier setbacks, had decided that they were not strong enough to achieve a landing, and he backed them in this decision.[8]

On the 8th October Churchill reported on Dakar to a tense and anxious House of Commons. Anyone expecting him to impute blame to de Gaulle for the failure was disappointed. In the course of his speech he stoutly proclaimed his and the Government's unshaken confidence in the Free French leader. 'I think his judgment has been extremely sure-footed,' he declared, 'and our opinion of him has been enhanced by everything we have seen of his conduct in circumstances of peculiar and perplexing difficulty. His Majesty's Government have no intention whatever of abandoning the cause of General de Gaulle until it is merged, as merged it will be, in the larger cause of France.' The responsibility for the *débâcle* Churchill attributed to the unforeseen appearance of the Vichy warships with their determined Vichy 'partisans.' He also spoke darkly of the 'accidents and errors'—even then the subject of disciplinary action or formal inquiry—which had prevented the First Sea Lord and the Cabinet being informed of the approach of the ships to Gibraltar until it was too late.[9]

Inevitably the Dakar failure involved not only de Gaulle but his whole movement. His associates in London found themselves under a cloud of hostility, tarred with the same brush as their leader. On the 1st October de Gaulle sent Muselier a long memorandum explaining the failure and outlining his immediate plans. This may have helped to reassure his followers and strengthen any wavering allegiance. But elsewhere reactions were different. Muselier, visiting the Liverpool camps where French servicemen were awaiting repatriation, met a strong anti-Gaullist mood. A number of naval officers, shocked by the bloodshed at Dakar, refused an invitation to dine with him. These men would return to France to spread the story of the Dakar 'atrocity' and increase the disaffection for de Gaulle.

Meanwhile, at Freetown, Cunningham—unhappily immobilized by an attack of gout—had been piecing together the confused facts of Operation Menace. He called Spears over to the *Barham* to help. He expressed to him the 'mild grouse' that the French had gone in too soon on the first morning, though he admitted this made no difference. He also asserted that the French transports had never approached nearer than six miles of Rufisque—a charge that Spears vigorously contested—and that according to his own liaison officers no French troops had landed there (which was almost certainly true). In the midst of this glum post-mortem Cunningham's CSO, Captain Walter, brought the report of a naval officer just arrived by flying-boat from England that—as they already knew only too well—'the effect of Dakar on English and American opinion had been absolutely disastrous.'[10]

For de Gaulle there was one crumb of comfort in the dismal picture. Reports now reached him indicating more Gaullist support in Dakar than had appeared at the time. The Gorée batteries, it was said, had never tried to hit the Allied ships. It was even hinted that the Vichy cruisers had deliberately refrained from engaging the Free French transports at Rufisque. An RAF officer from the *Ark Royal* had the impression that at least some of the French airmen at Ouakam were pro-Gaullist. The Dakar authorities had shown their fear of a Gaullist rising by placing machine-guns to command the town. Three citizens from Dakar declared the bombardment had aroused no resentment as it was thought inevitable after the envoys had been fired on. And—as encouragement for Cunningham—the accuracy of the British fire was praised, and the presence of the fog deplored as it was felt that had the Allied armada been visible it would have created an 'enormous impression.'

The question was now academic—but could clear weather (normally almost a certainty at that season) have altered the whole situation by revealing the assembled might of the Allied armada and thus inducing the Dakar authorities, having regard to the potential Gaullist sympathy within the town, to admit de Gaulle without resistance?

In the stagnant heat of Freetown de Gaulle was in constant conference with Cunningham and Spears and impatiently awaiting a pointer to his next move. This materialized on the 29th, in a cable from Nigeria announcing that Larminat was on his way from Brazzaville to Lagos and urgently required him there. But there was still the question of transport. By a stroke of luck a flying-boat from England arrived that day at Freetown, outward bound and carrying no passengers. This was de Gaulle's chance. Early next day he boarded the plane with de Courcel and one aide, bound for Lagos. After meeting Larminat at Lagos he went on to Duala in the Cameroons, to be warmly greeted there on the 9th October. Dakar was now behind him. Ahead, in French Equatorial Africa and elsewhere, lay fresh projects that were to bring him greater success and partially at least redeem the effect of that reverse.

No time was now lost in dispersing the Menace armada from Freetown. The Navy was wanted for other business and the Free French had further tasks in Africa. At the start of October the *Barham* and *Ark Royal* returned to Britain for repairs or refit. The crippled *Resolution* was towed to Gibraltar, while the Gibraltar-based Force H left with the British transports for the Azores to counter a possible German attack on the Canary Islands, and then on the 4th returned with them to Gibraltar. As for the Free French ships, on the 3rd the *Westernland* and

Pennland sailed for Victoria in the British Cameroons, escorted by the cruiser *Devonshire*. The supply ships went direct to Duala, in the French Cameroons, arriving there on the 13th. And early in November three of these were to proceed to Libreville (French Equatorial Africa) with a contingent of native and Foreign Legion troops. The Spears Mission, its immediate assignment ended, sailed in the *Westernland* and *Pennland* to Victoria. Its final destination, reached early in November, was Brazzaville on the Congo, which became the Mission's headquarters in Africa. The last meeting between Cunningham, de Gaulle and Spears was at Duala soon after de Gaulle's arrival there on the 9th, to frame a plan for de Gaulle's capture of Libreville.

For the moment de Gaulle's and Spears' association was over. De Gaulle had much reason to be grateful to Edward Spears. On the general's first arrival in England, virtually unknown to the British, Spears had been his sole champion. He had pressed his cause in official quarters and fought hard for his proper recognition as an ally to be reckoned with. And though they had not always agreed, Spears had backed him from the first in his plans for Dakar, had been a valued confidant and adviser, and sided with him on those prickly occasions when he clashed with the British commanders. (Spears' counsel was not always sound, as when he supported de Gaulle in his refusal to join the commanders on the flagship on the voyage to Freetown.) Now, while de Gaulle consolidated his position in Africa, their paths would part. But the two would meet again, when the Spears Mission was working in the Levant. Thereafter their relations would become less happy, and a final break between them was to come when they differed irreconcilably over the status of the Levant states. 'But that,' as Spears says, 'is another story.'

In Dakar itself, whatever the feelings of the civilians, the men on the ships had been celebrating a famous victory. The *Richelieu*'s officers had fêted the captain of the submarine *Beveziers* and the commander at Ouakam airfield with songs and toasting. It was in the *Richelieu* that the spirit of defiance that had 'seen off' the Allied armada was most evident. 'The *Richelieu* has suffered German bombs, English torpedoes, English gun-fire,' said one officer. 'We have fought three times. If we had to fight a fourth, fifth, tenth time, the *Richelieu* is ready to do it with the same devotion and the same confidence in the destiny of France.'[11] Ashore, the official jubilation was tempered by mourning for the dead. Early in October a solemn memorial service was held in the cathedral, attended by the service chiefs and the Governor-General.

Boisson was gratified by the messages that had poured in to congratulate him. But he expressed bitter resentment against de Gaulle's 'treasonous' conduct and the hostile propaganda that accused him of fighting for the Germans. 'No need,' he declared to a friend, 'for Laval to claim the advantage of the defence of Dakar for his pro-German policy. This opposition we've just put up against the British fleet doesn't at all mean that we would start hostilities against the neighbouring British colonies. Let that be well known at Vichy!'[12]

But while fully occupied with defending Dakar against the Allies, Boisson had narrowly escaped the added complication of German intervention there. At that very moment the Germans, showing a sudden interest in the West African capital, were preparing to send an 'economic' mission to Dakar. On the 24th September Vichy's Foreign Ministry was notified that a German mission was leaving by plane for Dakar. On the 25th the first plane, carrying three German 'economists', of whom one was an army colonel, arrived at Casablanca. Vichy at once telegraphed the German commission headquarters at Wiesbaden refusing them admission to Dakar, and Governor-General Noguès, at Casablanca, was ordered to forbid the plane flying on. The German 'economists' protested and insisted on going to Dakar, even disguised as tourists. But the Vichy Government, though realizing its weak position and the risks it was taking in defying its German masters, remained determined. On the 27th it cabled Noguès, maintaining its veto against the mission; and at the same time notified the commission's head at Wiesbaden, General von Stulpnagel, in strong but diplomatic terms that the Germans could not be admitted to Dakar. Impressed by Vichy's firmness, Stulpnagel called off the mission.[13]

This was a triumph for France's policy of keeping Germany out of her colonies at all costs. In that at least the Vichy Government was unanimous. But in other things it was deeply divided. In the aftermath of Dakar this was being impressed on Sir Samuel Hoare, in Madrid, by Vichy's Ambassador, de la Baume. Darlan and Laval, said de la Baume, detested each other but were agreed on one thing: their hatred of Britain. Baudouin, on the other hand, was striving to avoid a breach with either the Germans or the British. Hoare had evidence of this just after the abandonment of Menace. On the 26th—the day he wrote in puzzlement to Lord Halifax, 'I am very much bewildered by what has been happening in Dakar and perhaps you could send me a line some time to give me the background of it all'—he received notice of what amounted to an ultimatum, doubtless originating from Darlan.[14] Vichy had decided, he was told, to retake her defecting colonies and use the French Navy for convoying French merchant ships, and if the British intervened there would be war between the two countries.

But next day de la Baume, briefed by Baudouin, had a long talk with him aimed at improving Anglo-French relations. And on the 29th Baudouin made new proposals to Hoare, 'led to do so by the madness of this attack on Dakar, which . . . might cause Germany with the help of Italy to extend her field of action to the Western Mediterranean.'[15] He urged Britain to take a realistic view, in order to avoid such unfortunate incidents as that of Dakar, which were bound to please Germany. If the Dakar attempt was causing grave concern to Baudouin it was highly embarrassing to Hoare also. As he wrote to Halifax, it seemed to show once again Britain's incapacity to carry through any military plan. All he could do, he added, was to try to convince Baudouin that the operation showed Britain's wish to avoid intervention except where it was the clear desire of the population. Hoare may or may not have been aware what a weak argument this was in the case of Dakar. But what was now uncomfortably apparent to him and the politicians in London was that Operation Menace had, by its failure, created a highly delicate situation for both Britain and Vichy France.

What would have happened if Menace had succeeded is a matter for speculation. It is possible that the whole of French West and Equatorial Africa, encouraged by the fall of Dakar, might have gone over to de Gaulle. With Britain commanding the seas, Hitler could hardly have prevented this. He might have proceeded to occupy all France, but this would have been a heavy military commitment and alienated Vichy France still further, at a time when he wanted its co-operation. Would he, alternatively, have ignored French feelings and attempted to seize French North Africa? This, it seems, might have happened, as shown by a significant conversation that Vichy France's General Huntziger had with two generals from Hitler's General Staff in November 1940. The Germans confessed that the Dakar attempt had acutely alarmed the staff, and added that if it had succeeded they would immediately have gone into North Africa. 'If you French are not capable of defending French Africa,' they said, 'we will immediately carry war to that continent.'[16] All this is problematical. What can be said is that success at Dakar might have been a mixed blessing for the Allies. The setback to British and Free French morale incurred by the failure of Menace, serious though it was, has to be measured against the possible risk of the spreading of the war that its success would have produced.

As the smoke of Dakar cleared, one repercussion of it reached out to Gibraltar, the Rock past which the Vichy cruisers had sailed unchallenged on 11th September. It was convenient to blame the failure of Operation Menace largely on the unexpected appearance of the cruisers at Dakar. But with all the furore and condemnation that that failure had aroused in Britain and beyond, there had to be an individual scapegoat for it. De Gaulle had paid the price in a broader way, but that was not enough. On a more tactical level there was another likely victim. That victim was found in the person of Admiral North, C-in-C Atlantic Station, resident at Gibraltar, the man who had allegedly let the cruisers through. By way of an epilogue to the Dakar Affair, the scapegoating of North makes an unhappy story.

For a month after the abandonment of Menace, North had heard little of the Dakar business or the Vichy cruisers. Then, on the evening of 22nd October, he was in his study at The Mount when a 'safe hand' (personally officer-delivered) letter was brought him. It was from Their Lordships of the Admiralty, dated a week before and relating to the passage of the cruisers. He read through it, to reach the last—and operative—paragraph: 'Their Lordships cannot retain full confidence in an officer who fails in an emergency to take all prudent precautions without waiting for Admiralty instructions. They have accordingly decided that you should be relieved of your command at the first opportunity.' Flabbergasted, North telephoned Admiral Somerville, in harbour on his flagship *Renown*, to tell him of the signal and ask him to come and discuss it. Somerville arrived furious. Together they thrashed the matter out into the small hours. On leaving, Somerville (as North records) declared: 'Something stinks here. They can't do this to you. They're blaming you for what happened at Dakar.'[17]

But on the Admiralty books there was something else against Admiral North. On the previous 4th July, shocked at the ruthlessness of the Mers-el-Kebir episode, he had signalled a strong protest to the Admiralty. On the 17th a reply had come, drafted by the First Sea Lord, Sir Dudley Pound: '. . . The contents of your letter show a most dangerous lack of appreciation of the manner in which it is intended to conduct the war.' From that moment North's fate appears to have been sealed.

The Admiralty's dismissal letter of 15th October charged that North should have acted on information received to stop the French ships, as they might have been bound for a Nazi-held port; that he had been slow to pass on a signal to Somerville's Force H; that he should have ordered Force H to sea, even though it was under Admiralty orders. Somerville, himself officially exonerated (though he appeared to be as responsible as North for any errors or misjudgments allegedly committed during the period in question), vehemently backed North. In an effort to establish the facts, together they exhaustively checked over signals, orders, dates and times. But neither could see where North had gone wrong. In particular he had meticulously followed Admiralty standing instructions: 'Contact with equal or superior French forces should be avoided (9th July).' 'Government reserves the right to take action in regard to French warships proceeding to enemy-occupied ports (12th July).'

Among his service colleagues on the Rock there was widespread sympathy for North. Churchill's Commons speech about Dakar on 8th October, with its reference to 'a series of accidents and some errors' which were 'the subject of disciplinary action or formal inquiry' had done little to clarify matters, and North's staff officers strongly suspected their chief was being victimized for some gross blunder in Whitehall. Late that month Gibraltar's Governor, General Sir Clive Liddell, took up the cudgels for him by sending an indignant protest to the CIGS in London. But to no avail.

Back in London in January 1941, relieved of his command, North was to press the Admiralty for a court-martial. Sir Dudley Pound, First Sea Lord, curtly refused. And the First Lord, A. V. Alexander, was equally adamant. Referring to Oran, Alexander told him (significantly, as it was later to turn out): 'You know, North, you should never have written that letter.' So, at 59, after 44 years' service in which he had steadily climbed the naval ladder, to be mentioned latterly as a possible First Sea Lord, North's career was ruined. He was never to hold another important appointment, and all subsequent appeals he was to make for an investigation into his conduct were to be turned down. Grateful for the support of staunch friends like Lord Louis Mountbatten and King George VI himself, North looked for final vindication to the man he felt could really clear him—Winston Churchill. But this was not forthcoming.

In 1947 he was to meet Churchill at a Royal Navy Club dinner. The Dakar Affair was mentioned, and Churchill promised to look into North's case. North sent him all the signals and other material covering it which he had religiously collected and preserved, but received only a brief acknowledgment. And when Churchill's volume of war history, *Their Finest Hour*, appeared in 1949, all it admitted was that North was 'not in the Dakar circle and took no special action.' Churchill went on to explain away the Gibraltar *débâcle* as due to the signals confusion in Whitehall, caused by air-raids and the inefficiency of an Operations officer.

From 1940 onwards the Navy was never to cease championing North. He was seen as the biggest victim of injustice since Admiral Byng. But the service observed its traditional silence until, in October 1948, Rear-Admiral H. G. Thursfield spoke out in the *National Review*. Laying the blame for the passage of the Vichy cruisers squarely on 'the authorities at home', Thursfield called for the clearing of North's name. But the powers-that-be were to remain unmoved. And then, in 1953, came what might be called a salvo from the Navy's biggest guns of all. That May four Admirals of the Fleet, their spokesman Lord Chatfield, presented the First Lord, Mr J. P. L. Thomas, with a memorandum on the affair and requested an Inquiry. In essence their plea was that, at worst, North had shown an error of judgment and that there was no 'neglect of duty'. But this too was refused.

However, the following year brought North clear vindication from an unimpeachable source. The distinguished naval historian, Captain Stephen Roskill, in his official *History of the War at Sea*, came down firmly in the admiral's defence. And, with access to all the relevant records of the Gibraltar episode, Roskill was able to give an authoritative verdict. He wrote: 'The truth is that the chain of command was ill-defined and that such vagueness, besides being operationally dangerous, placed the responsible officers in an unfair position.'[18] The exoneration was hailed in the Navy and elsewhere (though bitterly attacked in some official quarters), but it failed equally to produce North's hoped-for Inquiry. The final veto came in 1957 when, with the matter raised in the House of Commons, the Prime Minister, Harold Macmillan, offered only the scant comfort that North could not be accused of dereliction of duty.

When North died in 1961, *The Times* printed a leader about

him, headed 'A Wartime Scapegoat.' But why he alone, without Somerville, who on his own admission was equally 'culpable', was picked for official condemnation remained a mystery until the recent release of secret Admiralty Papers gave the answer. Soon after Mers-el-Kebir the First Lord of the Admiralty, A. V. Alexander, received this letter from No. 10 Downing Street, dated 20th July 1940: 'It is evident that Admiral Dudley North has not got the root of the matter in him, and I should be very glad to see you replace him by a more resolute and clear-sighted officer.' The letter was signed: 'W. S. C.'[19]

Admiral North was clearly a marked man from the moment he had registered his protest about the Oran action. After that it was only a matter of finding the pretext to dismiss him. It should be said that under the Queen's Regulations Their Lordships of the Admiralty have the right to retire any officer without giving a reason. But in North's case the Silent Service was a hard taskmaster.

So the Dakar Affair has echoed on, almost to this day. The irony of it is that even if North had been guilty of a neglect of duty in letting the Vichy cruisers through, the cruisers had never been intended to reinforce Dakar's defences and never would have been at Dakar during Operation Menace, if Cunningham's force had not chased them back to that port when they were attempting to sail south to Libreville. The reasons for the failure of Operation Menace lie very much elsewhere than in the appearance of the Vichy cruisers or in what happened at Gibraltar on the 11th September, 1940.*

---

* But one intriguing question about the Vichy cruisers remains. Was Whitehall's delay in answering North's signals about them deliberate? This is the suggestion of the French writer, Jacques Mordal (*La Bataille de Dakar*, Paris. 1956, p. 129). Mordal theorizes that the War Cabinet, calculating that the French squadron, by its sortie into the Atlantic, might be escaping seizure by the Axis and thereby depriving the enemy of six valuable warships, could have decided to wait until the intentions of the squadron were clear. If it was eluding German control, the Cabinet's failure to answer North would not matter. If on the other hand the Cabinet's calculation was wrong and the ships were discovered to be bound on some Vichy mission, then the blame for letting them through the Straits could be thrust upon the man on the spot—the unlucky Admiral North.

CHAPTER XIV

CONCLUSION

The Dakar expedition, as Sir Samuel Hoare aptly commented, 'was one of these risky operations of war that are justified by success and condemned by failure.'[1] There was so much against it from the start that it would have been remarkable if it had succeeded. Politically, it was inherently a gamble. No one knew how Vichy, or Germany, would react if they got wind of it. Militarily, it was a complicated combined operation for which there was virtually no precedent apart from the abortive Gallipoli and Norway expeditions of 1915 and April 1940. Moreover it was conducted thousands of miles from its home base, and its international character presented added problems. And it was hurriedly mounted at a time of great difficulty for Britain, when the Government was heavily preoccupied with the invasion threat and resources, after Dunkirk, were scarce. But in addition to these basic handicaps there were various other factors that virtually doomed Menace to failure.

Contrary to widely held belief, the notorious information leakages played no part in this. The careless talk in bars and restaurants, de Gaulle's own indiscreet remarks while buying tropical kit in a Piccadilly outfitters, were certainly enough to alert the French, as were the troop and military traffic movements in late August. There were also those bizarre eve-of-departure accidents at Euston station and elsewhere, when bales of leaflets addressed to the citizens of Dakar were showered

178

around for everyone to see. On the other hand, much of this could have been taken to be part of a careful cover plan. In fact (as previously noted) no word of warning seems to have got back to Vichy, and on all the evidence Pétain and his colleagues remained unaware of any impending action against Dakar. But in this leakage myth there was a more sinister element, the suggestion of actual treachery involving de Gaulle's controversial and not always amenable deputy Admiral Muselier. In December Muselier was arrested and detained on the charge of passing the Dakar plans to Vichy. He was released soon after, with apologies from the Government, on the discovery that the documents inculpating him were forged—probably, it was said, by British Intelligence. The accusation was patently baseless, and most likely a rather unsavoury plot to discredit or sow discord among the Free French.

Nor did the Vichy cruisers contribute to Menace's failure. Their mission had nothing to do with defending Dakar, and if two of them had not been chased back to Dakar by Cunningham's force they would not have been there when the operation was launched. Moreover, these cruisers did not add significantly to Dakar's defensive strength. The factors that did to a greater or lesser degree ensure the operation's failure were: fog; bad communications; faulty top-command organization; and overoptimistic assessment of Gaullist support within Dakar. Taken separately, any one of these was enough to endanger success, but together they made it impossible.

The fog or thick haze which prevailed during the first two days of Menace had a three-fold result. It rendered the assembled strength of the Allied armada largely invisible from the shore (thus nullifying the psychological effect that the sight of it might have had on the citizens and garrison of Dakar); it prevented accurate bombardment and spotting by Cunningham's ships; and it created confusion among the armada itself by hiding the ships from each other and thus hampering coordinated movement. Spears and his colleagues were shocked to learn that fog was said to be a common occurrence on the West African coast at that season, and thought it incredible that the naval authorities were unprepared for it. Churchill on the other hand—and with more justification—attributes its presence to sheer bad luck. For before the operation the Air Ministry meteorologists had studied climatic conditions for the area during September and found that clear bright weather was normally assured.

But even without the fog there would have been trouble with ship-to-ship liaison. The operation was continually compromised by the glaring inefficiency of the communications. With signals not received, being misunderstood, delayed in transmission or decoding, or coming in too thick and fast to be handled properly, time and again the system was near to breakdown. Often at critical moments Cunningham and de Gaulle failed to make contact with each other, and neither knew where the other was or what he was doing. Vital orders went astray or were acted on long after they had ceased to be relevant. Urgent questions were left unanswered. De Gaulle had his own personal worry in the omission to embark the special long-range set with which he was to communicate with London. The general communications chaos was at least as instrumental as fog in frustrating the success of Menace.

Defective top-command organization played a major part in the failure. First, on the voyage to Freetown de Gaulle had made an outstanding blunder in refusing to join the British commanders on the flagship. He was thus isolating himself from immediate contact and consultation with Cunningham and Irwin, and slowing-down vital decision-making during the operation, to rely instead on ship-to-ship communication that was to prove so ineffective. But apart from this there was the omission to provide what was a necessity for a combined operation like Menace: a Headquarters ship. From such a vessel Cunningham and Irwin (with de Gaulle) would have been free to direct their forces without being involved in minute-to-minute tactical changes or sudden emergency movements. The omission had become obvious when Cunningham and Irwin had found themselves chasing around the Atlantic on the purely tactical mission of rounding up the Vichy cruisers, instead of remaining at Freetown on a combined Headquarters ship. Furthermore, an HQ vessel would have assured proper space and working facilities for the staff, sparing them the chaotic makeshift conditions they had to endure on the *Devonshire* and *Barham*.

To General Irwin the lack of an HQ ship had been woefully apparent before and during the operation. More than once he had been forced, to his profound annoyance, to sail off in an opposite direction to the transports carrying his troops. He stressed the matter strongly in his own report on Menace, and lecturing on Dakar in 1941 he was to recall: 'On two occasions the combined staffs were broken up, first when we went north at 30 knots to intercept the French squadron, and later, when the Naval Commander went off again to chase the French units and I was left ashore.' On the role of the Naval Commander, he added: 'If [he is] flying his flag in a ship of the operating fleet, the admiral cannot but command that fleet. He will not lightly hand over the command of the fighting squadron to someone else and sit back. If the Joint Command is to function as such . . . he must be relieved of the responsibility of also fighting his ships.'[2]

Most serious of all, however, was the false estimate of the extent of Gaullist support in Dakar. The whole Menace project had been based on the belief that de Gaulle would be welcomed there, with perhaps only token resistance and minimum blood-shed (though provision had later been made to force a landing if necessary). Many reports had seemed to confirm this assessment. But most were completely misleading as to the effectiveness of the support in actually aiding a Gaullist take-over. They had also gravely underestimated the Vichy sympathies of the authorities and the fighting spirit and defensive strength of the Dakar forces. Larminat's warning had been ignored and the most realistic report, that of Commander Rushbrooke and Captain Poulter, had—fatefully—come too late to be considered as it deserved.

The War Office authorities virtually admitted this. 'Actually Captain Poulter's estimate of the probable defences,' it was later officially stated, 'received verbally only on the eve of sailing, *proved in the end fairly accurate* (author's italics), but in complete absence of confirmation, if not of contradiction from other sources well qualified to judge, his estimate was only partially accepted by the Force Commanders.'[3]

The Rushbrooke-Poulter statement holds a key place in the whole affair. Had it been available earlier, in time for its implications to be fully weighed, it is fair to assume that Operation Menace would never have taken place. Rushbrooke and Poulter had been ordered to return home on the 10th August, when planning for Menace was in a preliminary stage and up-to-date information on which to base it was urgently wanted. If they had arrived back within 48 hours or so with their report, it must have been acknowledged that Menace stood no chance of success. Further preparation on it could then have been abandoned before the commitment to it had become too deep. But the last-minute return of the two officers, within hours of the convoy's departure, made acceptance of their report and consequent abandonment virtually impossible. Menace had to go ahead, even though it was a lost cause.

Official sensitivity about the matter is shown in a significant way. In the Official Report on Menace, pasted over a footnote referring to the Rushbrooke-Poulter statement is a typed amendment commenting: 'It is perhaps permissible to point out that Commander Rushbrooke and Captain Poulter had been summoned to produce facts about the defences so that the details of the plan could be completed, and that Captain Poulter's statement about the spirit of the defenders may well have been regarded as a matter of opinion.'[4]

The outcome of Menace was to show how valid that opinion was.

Other shortcomings that jeopardized Menace's success were: hurried planning and preparation owing to shortness of time; hasty collection of staff; sketchy training for possible landing operations; superiority of Vichy aircraft and inadequacy of Allied assault landing craft. But after the war General Irwin was to cite two more factors that he thought important. The first involved a tactical error: the British decision to advertise Allied intentions beforehand instead of carrying out surprise landings on the beaches, where a welcome could have been expected from the bulk of the population despite some military opposition. Secondly there was a psychological error in allowing the operation to start with a broadcast from de Gaulle. As de Gaulle was only a brigadier-general his superior officers ashore were— in accordance with the traditional French respect for seniority —likely to resent being given 'orders' by a subordinate. Further, Irwin stressed the dilemma in which the Joint Commanders were placed. They were to try persuasion backed by the display, but not the use, of force. And then, if a favourable response was not forthcoming, they were directed to employ all the force available. But in fact this force was not enough to overcome a determined defence.[5]

Irwin pointed to various problems confronting the Menace planners. For instance, should Menace be regarded solely as a military operation, whose aim was to seize an objective irrespective of the feelings of the defenders? Could a peaceful landing be made without some expectation of co-operation from the defence? Or again, was it fair to ask armed troops to land on the understanding that they would be unopposed, and then place them in a position of extreme disadvantage if they were opposed? Such questions had to be answered in the final planning by a compromise, 'which, no doubt, prejudiced the prospects of success.'

Judged by the benefit of hindsight, Operation Menace seemed pre-destined to fail. It was planned and prepared in the face of doubts and difficulties, beset by mishaps and bad luck, and carried out against heavy odds. From a rational viewpoint it should never have been staged at all. But it has to be seen in the context of the summer of 1940. In those dark days when France lay defeated except for the activity of the small, newly founded Free French movement led by General de Gaulle, such an operation was the Allies' sole means of showing they could strike back, other than by not very formidable RAF bombing.

It was therefore a courageous bid to keep the British flag flying and plant a new one. And, strategically, Dakar was an objective well worth gaining if there had been a reasonable chance of doing so with the resources at the Allies' disposal.

In fact the chance was there—within a hair's-breadth of realization. One of Admiral Cunningham's stated reasons for finally withdrawing on the morning of the 25th September was that 'the possibility of enemy ammunition being nearly exhausted was not confirmed.' In this he had fatefully miscalculated. As the British fleet retired in defeat that morning after the crippling of the *Resolution*, Dakar was on the point of giving in. This startling revelation was made by Pierre Boisson, the Governor-General, to Cunningham when they met towards the end of the war. Boisson confessed to Cunningham that during that last British attack, his own ships and forts had almost run out of ammunition and he was in the act of writing out a message of surrender.[6] That message was never sent. Dakar had been saved by the narrowest margin—by the homing torpedo of the *Beveziers*. Many ironies had marked the course of Operation Menace, but this was the biggest one of all.

REFERENCES

Chapter I.
1. Spears, Sir E. *Two Men who Saved France*, 1966. p. 147.
2. Spears Diary.
3. Spears. p. 177.
4. Cabinet Papers CAB 65/14, 23.
5. Passy. *Souvenirs*, Vol. 1, 1947. p. 41.
6. Ibid.
7. Grinnell-Milne, D. *The Triumph of Integrity*, 1961. p. 125.
8. Butler, J. R. M. *Grand Strategy*, Vol. 2, 1957. p. 312.
9. Churchill, W. S. *Their Finest Hour*, 1949. p. 420.
10. Cabinet Papers CAB 65/14, 74.
11. De Gaulle, C. *The Call to Honour*, 1955. pp. 120–122.
12. Cabinet Papers CAB 79/6.
13. Admiralty Papers ADM 199/906.
14. Ibid.
15. Cabinet Papers CAB 65/14, 96.
16. Admiralty Papers ADM 199/906.

Chapter II.
1. Muselier, E. H. *De Gaulle contre le Gaullisme*, 1946. p. 77.
2. Soustelle, J. *Envers et contre Tout*, 1947. p. 140.
3. Cabinet Papers CAB 79/6.
4. Churchill. p. 424.
5. Grinnell-Milne. pp. 129–130.
6. Admiralty Papers ADM 199/907.
7. Churchill. p. 423.
8. Admiralty Papers ADM 199/907.
9. Cabinet Papers CAB 79/6.

10. Admiralty Papers ADM 199/907.
11. Ibid.
12. Cabinet Papers CAB 65/14, 116.
13. Admiralty Papers ADM 199/906.
14. Ibid. ADM 199/907.
15. Ibid.
16. Ibid.
17. Ibid.

Chapter III.
  1. Spears Diary.
  2. Jenkins Letter.
  3. De Gaulle. p. 123.
  4. Spears Diary.
  5. Ibid.
  6. Admiralty Papers ADM 199/906.
  7. Mitchell Diary.
  8. Ibid.
  9. St John, J. *To the War with Waugh*, 1973. p.42.
 10. Spears Diary.

Chapter IV.
  1. Roskill, S. W. *The War at Sea*, 1954. pp. 309–310.
  2. Churchill. p. 425.
  3. Admiralty Papers ADM 199/907.
  4. Spears Papers.
  5. Ibid.
  6. Spears Diary.
  7. Mordal, J. *La Bataille de Dakar*, 1956. p. 131.
  8. Jameson, W. *Ark Royal 1939–41*, 1957. p. 283

Chapter V.
  1. Wingate, Sir R. *Not in the Limelight*, 1959. p. 165.

2. Higham Letter.
3. Mitchell Diary.
4. Bryant, Sir A. *The Turn of the Tide 1939–1943*, 1957. pp. 215, 217.
5. Ibid. p. 216.
6. Churchill. p. 426.
7. Cabinet Papers CAB 65/9 WM (40), 250.
8. Ibid. CAB 65/15, 17.
9. Churchill. p. 427.
10. Cadogan, Sir E. *The Diaries 1938–1945*, 1971. p. 327.
11. Churchill. p. 428.
12. Spears Diary.
13. Spears Papers.
14. Ibid.
15. Churchill. pp. 428–429.
16. Cabinet Papers CAB 65/15, 21.
17. Ibid. CAB 65/15, 23.
18. Cadogan. p. 327.
19. Cabinet Papers CAB 65/15, 23.
20. Admiralty Papers ADM 199/907.
21. Churchill. p. 249.
22. Ibid. pp. 429–430.
23. Ibid. p. 430.
24. Spears Papers.

Chapter VI.
1. Spears Diary.
2. Ibid.
3. Spears Papers.
4. Jameson. pp. 206–207.
5. Spears Diary.
6. De Gaulle. p. 125.
7. Churchill. p. 430.
8. Mordal. p. 133.
9. Spears Diary.

Chapter VII.
1. Mordal. p. 140.
2. Ibid. pp. 307–308.
3. Ibid. p. 141.
4. Admiralty Papers ADM 199/907.
5. Mordal. p. 147.
6. Ibid. p. 148.
7. Baudouin, P. *The Private Diaries (March 1940–Jan. 1941)*, p. 243.
8. Churchill. p. 431.
9. Ibid. p. 432.
10. Mitchell Diary.
11. Jameson. p. 207.

Chapter VIII.
1. Mordal. p. 164.
2. Ibid. pp. 160–161.
3. Martin du Gard, M. *La Carte Impériale*, 1949. pp. 105–106.
4. Laurent, J. *Année '40*, 1965. p. 333.
5. *France d'Abord*, No. 1, 12 Jan. 1941.
6. Soustelle. p. 144.
7. *France d'Abord*.
8. Laurent. pp. 374–377.
9. Baudouin. p. 237.
10. Ibid. p. 239.
11. Muselier. p. 85.
12. Soustelle. p. 147.
13. Foreign Office Papers PRE/3/276 p. 132.

Chapter IX.
1. Laurent. p. 350.
2. Spears Papers.
3. Rigg, J. B. 'The Battle of Dakar'. *Blackwood's Magazine*, March 1963, Vol. 293, pp. 193–208.

4. St John. p. 50.
5. HMS *Cumberland*. Action Record.
6. Mitchell Papers.
7. Laurent. p. 358.
8. Mitchell Diary.
9. Laurent. p. 359.
10. Mordal. p. 176.
11. Soustelle. p. 157.
12. HMS *Cumberland*. Action Record.
13. Spears. p. 197.

Chapter X.
1. Laurent. p. 359.
2. Ibid.
3. Ibid.
4. Rigg. pp. 199–201.
5. Admiralty Papers ADM 199/906.
6. Spears Papers.
7. Spears. p. 198.
8. Spears Papers.
9. Laurent. p. 359.
10. Mordal. p. 189.
11. Grinnell-Milne. p. 143.
12. Mordal. pp. 194–196.
13. Spears Papers.
14. Soustelle. p. 159.
15. Wingate. p. 168.
16. Admiralty Papers ADM 199/907.
17. Ibid.
18. Mitchell Diary.
19. Spears. p. 200.
20. Spears Papers.
21. Wingate. p. 168.
22. Mitchell Diary.
23. Spears Papers.
24. Admiralty Papers ADM 199/906.

25. Ibid. ADM 199/907.
26. Spears Papers.
27. Mitchell Diary.
28. Cadogan. p. 328.
29. Cabinet Papers CAB 65/9 WM(40), 256.
30. Baudouin. pp. 246–247.
31. Laurent. p. 368.
32. Admiralty Papers ADM 199/906.
33. Baudouin. p. 247.
34. *The Times*, 24 September 1940.
35. Rougier, L. *Mission Secrète à Londres*, 1947. p. 42.

Chapter XI.
 1. Laurent. p. 360.
 2. Mordal. pp. 199–200.
 3. Gallaway Letter.
 4. Admiralty Papers ADM 199/906.
 5. Laurent. p. 361.
 6. Mitchell Diary.
 7. St John. p. 52.
 8. Spears Diary and Papers.
 9. Spears. pp. 207–208.
10. Spears Diary and Papers.
11. De Gaulle. p. 132.
12. Admiralty Papers ADM 199/906.
13. Spears Diary.
14. Jameson. p. 128.
15. *The Times*, 24 September 1940.
16. Baudouin. p. 248.
17. Spears Papers.
18. Rougier. pp. 65–66.
19. Spears Diary.
20. Ibid.
21. Spears Papers.
22. Admiralty Papers ADM 199/906.

Chapter XII.

1. Churchill. p. 432.
2. Admiralty Papers ADM 199/907.
3. Rigg. p. 204.
4. Grinnell-Milne. p. 147.
5. Admiralty Papers ADM 199/906.
6. St John. p. 53.
7. Spears Diary and Papers.
8. Laurent. p. 362.
9. *The Times*, 25 September 1940.
10. Cabinet Papers CAB 65/15, 41.
11. Ibid.
12. Churchill. pp. 434-435.
13. Ibid. p. 435.
14. Baudouin. p. 249.
15. Ibid. pp. 249-250.
16. Ibid. p. 250.
17. Admiralty Papers ADM 199/907.
18. Spears Papers.
19. Spears Diary.
20. Spears Papers.
21. Spears Diary.

Chapter XIII.

1. Rigg. p. 207.
2. Jameson. p. 221.
3. De Gaulle. p. 133.
4. Spears Papers.
5. Ibid.
6. Ibid.
7. Spears Diary.
8. Churchill. p. 645.
9. Hansard Parliamentary Debates, Commons. 5th Series, Vol. 365, 1940. col. 298 *et seq.*
10. Spears Diary.
11. Martin du Gard. p. 127.

12. Ibid. p. 136.
13. Charles-Roux, F. *Cinq Mois Tragiques aux Affaires Etrangères*, 1949. pp. 333–334.
14. Hoare. p. 86.
15. Baudouin. p. 253.
16. Ibid.
17. Most of this account of the North Episode is taken from: Monks, N. *That Day at Gibraltar*, 1957.
18. Roskill. *The War at Sea*. p. 311.
19. Admiralty Papers. ADM 1/19177.

Chapter XIV.
 1. Hoare. p. 86.
 2. Admiralty Papers ADM 199/907.
 3. Ibid. ADM 199/906.
 4. Ibid. ADM 199/907.
 5. Irwin, N. M. S. Dakar. *Le Trait d'Union*, Vol. 7, No. 12, 1948. pp. 3–8.
 6. Saunders Papers.

SOURCES AND BIBLIOGRAPHY

A. Official Publications
Public Record Office.
  Cabinet Papers.
  Admiralty Papers.
  Foreign Office Papers.
Ministry of Defence, Naval Historical Branch.
  Naval Staff History, Second World War: Naval Operations off Dakar, July–September 1940. 1959.
  War Diary (Naval), September 1940.

B. Private Material
Spears, General Sir Edward L. Diary and Papers relating to Dakar Operation.
Mitchell, Major F. Diary and Papers relating to Dakar Operation.
Home Cook, Capt. H., R.N. (Retd.), Action Record, H.M.S. *Cumberland.*
Saunders, Cmdr M. G., R.N. Papers.
Letters and other material from participants in Dakar Operation.

C. Other Works
Annual Register, 1940. (London 1941)
Aron, Robert. *The Vichy Regime 1940–1944.* Transl. by Humphrey Hoare. (London 1958)
Atkins, Paul M. 'Dakar and the Strategy of West Africa'. *Foreign Affairs*, Vol. 20. (New York 1941)
Atkins, Paul M. 'French West Africa in Wartime'. *National Geographic Magazine*, Vol. 81. (New York 1942)

Baudouin, Paul. *The Private Diaries (March 1940–Jan 1941)*. Transl. by Sir Charles Petrie. (London 1948)

Bouthillier, Yves. *Le Drame de Vichy*. Vol. 1, Face à l'Ennemi, Face à l'Allié. (Paris 1950)

Bryant, Sir Arthur. *The Turn of the Tide, 1939–1943*. (London 1957)

Buckmaster, M. J. *Specially Employed*. (London 1952)

Butler, J. R. M. *Grand Strategy*. Vol. 2, Sep 1939–Jun 1941. (History of the Second World War: U.K. Military Series.) (London 1971)

Cadogan, Sir Edward. *The Diaries, 1938–1945*. Ed. by David Dilke. (London 1971)

Charles-Roux, F. *Cinq Mois Tragiques aux Affaires Etrangères (21 mai–1 novembre 1940)*. (Paris 1949)

Chenet, Daniel. *Qui a Sauvé l'Afrique?* (Paris 1949)

Churchill, Winston S. *Their Finest Hour (The Second World War, Vol. 2)*. (London 1949)

Cobban, Alfred. *A History of Modern France*. Vol. 3, 1871–1962). (Harmondsworth 1962)

Cole, Hubert. *Laval: a Biography*. (London 1963)

Crawley, Aidan. *De Gaulle: a Biography*. (London 1969)

Crozier, Brian. *De Gaulle*. Vol. I, The Warrior. (London 1973)

Davis, Forrest, and Lindley, Ernest K. *How War Came to America*. (London 1943)

De Gaulle, Charles. *War Memoirs*. Vol. I, The Call to Honour. Transl. by Jonathan Griffin. (London 1955)

Docteur, Vice-Admiral. *La Vérité sur les Amiraux*. (Paris 1949)

Fergusson, Bernard. *The Watery Maze: the Story of Combined Operations*. (London 1961)

Foote, M. R. D. *S. O. E. in France*. (History of the Second World War.) (London 1966)

France d'Abord, No. 1. (Brazzaville 1941)

Grinnell-Milne, Duncan. *The Triumph of Integrity: a Portrait of Charles de Gaulle*. (London 1961)

Hansard Parliamentary Debates, Commons. Sept–Oct 1940. (London 1940)

Hauge, E. O., and Hartmann, V. *Flight from Dakar*. (London 1954)

Heckstall-Smith, A. *The Fleet that Faced Both Ways*. (London 1963)

Hoare, Sir Samuel. *Ambassador on Special Mission*. (London 1946)

Hull, Cordell. *The Memoirs*. 2 vols. (London 1943)

Hytier, Adrienne Doris. *Two Years of French Foreign Policy, Vichy, 1940–42*. (Geneva and Paris 1958)

Irwin, N. M. S. Dakar. *Le Trait d'Union*, Vol. 7, No. 12. (West Africa 1948)

Jameson, William. *Ark Royal 1939–41*. (London 1957)

Kammerer, Albert. *La Passion de la Flotte Française: de Mers-el-Kebir à Toulon*. (Paris 1951)

Lacouture, Jean. *De Gaulle*. Transl. by Francis K. Price. (London 1970)

Larminat, Edgard de. *Chroniques Irrévérencieuses*. (Paris 1962)

Laurent, Jacques. *Année '40: Londres-de Gaulle-Vichy*. (Paris 1965)

McCallum, R. B. *England and France 1939–43*. (London 1944)

Martin du Gard, Maurice. *La Carte Impériale: Histore de la France Outre Mer*. (Paris 1949)

Monks, Noel. *That Day at Gibraltar*. (London 1957)

Moran, Lord (Sir Charles Wilson). *Winston Churchill: the Struggle for Survival*. (London 1968)

Mordal, Jacques. *La Bataille de Dakar*. (Paris 1956)

Muselier, Emile Henry. *De Gaulle contre le Gaullisme*. (Paris 1946)

Nicolson, Harold. *Diaries and Letters*. Vol. 2, 1939–45. (London 1967)

Passy, Col. (*pseud.*). *Souvenirs*. Vol. 1, *Deuxième Bureau Londres*. (Monte Carlo 1947)

Pendar, Kenneth. *Adventure in Diplomacy*. (London 1966)

Raphael, Lois A. C. Dakar and the Desert Road. *Political Science Quarterly*, Vol. 59, March 1944. (London 1944)

Rigg, J. B. 'The Battle of Dakar'. *Blackwood's Magazine*, Vol. 293, March 1963. (London 1963)

Roskill, Stephen W. *The War at Sea 1939–45*. Vol. 1. (History of the Second World War: UK Military Series: Campaigns.) (London 1954)

Roskill, Stephen W. *The Navy at War*. (London 1960)

Rougier, Louis. *Mission Secrète à Londres.* (Paris 1947)

Smith, Denys. *America and the Axis War.* (London 1942)

Soustelle, Jacques. *Envers et contre Tout.* (Paris 1947)

Spears, Sir Edward. *Two Men who Saved France: Pétain and de Gaulle.* (London 1966)

St John, John. *To the War with Waugh.* (London 1973)

Taylor, A. J. P. *English History 1914–1945.* (Harmondsworth 1970)

Thursfield, H. G. 'Pour Encourager les Autres: a Naval Episode of 1940'. *National Review*, October 1948. (London 1948)

Times, The. September 1940 *passim.*

Warner, Geoffrey. *Pierre Laval and the Eclipse of France.* (London 1968)

Watson, J. A. *L'Echec à Dakar.* Transl. by Daniel Martin. (Paris 1968)

Waugh, Evelyn. *Men at Arms.* (London 1952)

Wingate, Sir Ronald. *Not in the Limelight.* (London 1959)

Woodward, Sir Llewellyn. *British Foreign Policy in the Second World War.* (History of the Second World War: Miscellaneous Vols.) (London 1962)

INDEX

The nationality of vessels is shown unless British

Index